Changes in Attitudes to Immigrants in Britain, 1841–1921

Changes in Attitudes to Immigrants in Britain, 1841–1921

From Foreigner to Alien

Ben Braber

ANTHEM PRESS

Anthem Press
An imprint of Wimbledon Publishing Company
www.anthempress.com

This edition first published in UK and USA 2022
by ANTHEM PRESS
75–76 Blackfriars Road, London SE1 8HA, UK
or PO Box 9779, London SW19 7ZG, UK
and
244 Madison Ave #116, New York, NY 10016, USA

First published in the UK and USA by Anthem Press in 2021

Copyright © Ben Braber 2022

The author asserts the moral right to be identified as the author of this work.

All rights reserved. Without limiting the rights under copyright reserved above,
no part of this publication may be reproduced, stored or introduced into
a retrieval system, or transmitted, in any form or by any means
(electronic, mechanical, photocopying, recording or otherwise),
without the prior written permission of both the copyright
owner and the above publisher of this book.

British Library Cataloguing-in-Publication Data
A catalogue record for this book is available from the British Library.

ISBN-13: 978-1-83998-560-7 (Pbk)
ISBN-10: 1-83998-560-7 (Pbk)

Cover image: 'Alien Laws', *The Times* (London, England),
Wednesday, Aug 20, 1884; pg. 2; Issue 31217;
© Times Newspapers Limited

This title is also available as an e-book.

CONTENTS

List of Illustrations	vii
Preface to the 2022 Edition	ix
Introduction	1
1. The Meanings of Alien	17
2. Quantitative Analysis of the Use of Alien	31
3. Qualitative Analysis of the Use of Alien	47
Conclusion	89
Notes	95
Bibliography	111
Index	117

ILLUSTRATIONS

Figures

1. The frequency of the word alien in a corpus of British English literature, 1841–1921 — 34
2. The use of the words alien and aliens in Britain's parliament — 36
3. Trends in word choice in *The Times*, 1840–1919 — 45
4. The use and meaning of the word alien in *The Times*, 1841–1920 — 49
5. Meanings of the word alien in *The Times* — 52

Tables

1. Census totals and selected countries of birth of foreign-born persons in Britain, 1841–1921 — 6
2. The number of uses in the Google Books corpus of British English publications — 33
3. The number of uses in Britain's parliament according to Hansard — 35
4. The number of uses of specific words in British Library Nineteenth-Century British Pamphlets — 37
5. The number of uses of specific words in the British Newspaper Archive — 40
6. The number of uses of specific words in Nineteenth-Century British Library Newspapers — 41
7. Number of uses in selected British newspapers — 43
8. Number of uses in *The Times* and *Daily Mail* — 44
9. The use and meaning of the word alien in *The Times*, 1841–1920 — 48
10. Meanings of the word alien in *The Times*, 1841–1921 — 50

PREFACE TO THE 2022 EDITION

Immigration continues to be a subject of heated debate in academical, political and public life. In 2022, there is talk about a migration 'crisis' and even a cabinet 'clash' about immigration.[1]

Integration of immigrants and their descendants has been one of my main research interests ever since I graduated as a historian. In that research I define integration as a process through which a minority group becomes part of a society without necessarily losing the group's original identity and characteristics, and during which the wider society itself undergoes changes by absorbing the minority. Many factors can influence such a process, including the attitudes and behaviour of the general population towards members of the integrating group and their repercussions for the behaviour of that group. The speed and direction of this process can also depend on other factors, encompassing the cohesion of the integrating group and the wider society as well as the preparedness and readiness of the general population and the integrating group to undergo changes. Other factors include the economic, social, political and cultural developments of the society in which integration takes place. Furthermore, the education of children can help to determine the speed and course of integration. Some of these factors can influence each other, while others occur independently. There can be interaction as well as a lack of contact between the general population and members of the integrating group. The result is usually a multi-layered, non-linear and long-term process.

In this book I examine one of these factors in a particular setting: the changing attitudes to immigrants in Britain between 1841 and 1921. Currently racism, hate and discrimination continue to affect people from black, Asian and ethnic minority groups with immigrant backgrounds. Quite a few attitudes in the present general population towards immigrants hark back to emotions evoked between 1841 and 1921. These feelings, which are described in this book, probably became part of a collective memory and were conveyed from one generation to the next, to rise again repeatedly. However, people can change their attitudes and behaviour. So, I hope to have produced a case study that clarifies history and provides insights that prove useful in studying and supporting processes of integration that take place as human migration across the globe persists.

I express this hope with gratitude. I am grateful to the historians who went before me, my teachers and colleagues as well as my family and friends, plus all the helpful linguists, archivists, librarians, readers, reviewers and editors, without whom this book would not exist. It is impossible to name all these people and detail their contribution, but I pray that I have not disappointed them.

INTRODUCTION

A hundred years ago the official statisticians of the United Kingdom turned foreigners into aliens. The change transpired in the headings of table columns in printed reports of the kingdom's census that recorded the number of people who were present in the country and did not have the British nationality. In 1911 they had been classified as foreigners, but ten years later they were listed as aliens, leading, for example, to the heading 'Alien nationality (and nationality not stated)'.[1] However, the substitution was not implemented consistently across all reports; a census reporter stated in an introduction to the published figures on Nottingham: 'Foreigners born in Germany were 258 in 1911, and are now reduced to 65.'[2]

Perhaps the Nottingham reporter wanted to avoid using the word alien. From a post-1921 point of view – before alien generally acquired an additional new meaning as in extraterrestrial[3] – alien appears more hostile than foreigner and the word carries an antagonistic denotation.

The census change from foreigner to alien may have been an application of the prevailing legal terminology, as in 'an alien is a citizen of another country'. The Aliens Act of 1905 could have given rise to the term. However, that raises the question why the term was not applied in the 1911 census documents. The answer may be that a stronger impetus for change was needed. The First World War could have provided that momentum. As a result of the war and its outcomes, the British Nationality and Status of Aliens Act 1914, the Aliens Restriction (Amendment) Act 1919 and the Alien Order 1920 had come into force, emphasising the prevalence of alien in contemporary statutes.

On the other hand, the census change may also have arisen from the influence of a debate on immigration that preceded the 1905 Aliens Act, lasted well into the twentieth century and resurfaced in the twenty-first. The discourse grew in strength during the second half of the nineteenth century, when concerns rose about an increasing presence of immigrants in Britain. The debate used the word alien, and some participants voiced strong opinions on immigrants, which could have caused the census modification.

There is of course another possibility. The increased use of the word alien and the census alteration may also have reflected wider changes in the English language.

In order to determine what influenced the decision to substitute the names of categories used by the enumerators, this book explores the change from foreigner to alien in greater detail. This is achieved by applying a linguistic analysis in history, where word use is examined within a framework of changes in the language and the society where that language was used. By heading down this avenue of investigation and focusing on newspapers, this book presents a case study that exposes changes in attitudes to immigrants in Britain between 1841 and 1921 and reveals the altering use and meaning of the word alien that was used to voice these attitudes in this period.

Parameters

The period under review is 1841–1921. The starting date of 1841 is chosen because from that year the census, which took place every 10 years, recorded the presence of foreigners in Britain. The end year of 1921 is selected because after that year new media such as the radio made their inroads next to printed newspapers, which had until then been the main mass communication platforms that reflected and formed attitudes and mirrored and influenced language use. And, as stated above, after 1921 the term alien gained its new extraterrestrial meaning.

During these years the vast majority of the British Isles formed the United Kingdom of Great Britain and Ireland, but this book concentrates on Britain, the mainland of the Isles, which consisted of England, Wales and Scotland.

This book refers to other countries, notably when the main groups of foreign-born residents in Britain are discussed. They include Russia, Poland, Germany, France, Italy, the United States and China. The use of these country names is problematic. Poland did not exist as an independent state during the period under review. It had been partitioned and the parts had been annexed by the Kingdom of Prussia and the Russian and Austro-Hungary empires. However, census takers and other people who provided information for the census still used the name Poland; there were no clear guidelines and persons born in what had been Poland could be recorded as having been born in Poland, Russia or one of the other annexing states. Another problem is that some countries were not yet in existence in 1841.

To solve these issues, Russia and Poland are regarded here as one country, usually referred to as Russia or the Russian Empire, which, during the period under review, incorporated part of Poland and the present-day Baltic States: Lithuania, Latvia and Estonia. Germany means the German states that united in 1871 as the German Empire. France means the French kingdom, republics and empire that existed between 1841 and 1921. Italy means the Italian states that formed the Kingdom of Italy from 1861. The United States means the states that formed or became part of the United States of America between 1841 and 1921. China means the land area ruled by the Qing dynasty to 1912, when it became the Republic of China.

There were other foreign-born groups in Britain, but in the period under review they were smaller than the groups from the countries above. An exception was the large group of people who had been born in British colonies, dominions, dependencies and other territories. For example, in 1911 the census reported 161,502 people residing in Britain who had been born in British colonies and India.[4] There are problems in dealing with them as immigrants or aliens. For example, in census records they appear as people born outside Britain in the British Empire and residing in Britain on the census date. Among them were large numbers of people born abroad from British parents and emigrants from Britain who returned to their country of origin. These people were not regarded as immigrants. They had the British nationality, just as people born in most territories within the British Empire were British subjects, and as such, they were usually not perceived as aliens. For that reason this group has been omitted from this study.

However, where references found to specific groups of people from countries that supplied fewer immigrants to Britain than the ones mentioned above and the British imperial subjects, such as expressions of a perceived immigrant or alien nature, these are discussed in this book.

This book is not the first work to investigate the issues of immigration and language use. There is a vast body of work on the history of migration in Britain during the years between 1841 and 1921, and on attitudes towards immigrants in this period.[5] The history of the 1905 Aliens Act has also been described extensively.[6] However, some of this literature has suggested that the 1905 Act and other contemporary attempts at alien legislation in Britain as well as the public and political debates which accompanied these initiatives were aimed solely at Jewish immigrants.[7] This book re-addresses that issue and brings out which other groups of immigrants were affected and how these effects were caused by changing attitudes towards foreigners in Britain during the nineteenth century. Recently, new points of view on the 1905 Act and the colonial and international context of this law have been highlighted.[8] This book reviews these angles too.

Although the link between attitude and language remains to be fully explored in historical research, a corpus linguistic approach to the language of migration in the Victorian press has already been adopted.[9] This book uses a similar method to study large corpora of text to discern patterns in language use in a specific period and compare them to patterns in other periods. In addition, there is an extensive linguistic literature on changes in the English language during the second half of the nineteenth century and early years of the twentieth century. This book utilises a selection of these publications.[10]

In contrast with the available literature, this book binds it all together. It builds on and expands the historiography on migration with the dual purpose of shedding new light on the development of attitudes to immigrants and gaining a greater understanding of their integration into a modern West European society.

Context

This book examines the words that were used to write and talk about immigrants within a context of changes in the British society. During the period under review Britain went through numerous developments that altered people's lives, had started earlier and continued after 1921. This book is not the place to provide a comprehensive overview of all changes.[11] However, it covers a period of 80 years, during which a fundamental transformation took place, and that necessitates longer than usual preliminary remarks about some of the changes that shaped the background against which attitudes towards immigrants were formed and language developed. This section highlights these changes before the remainder of the introduction focuses on sources and methodology.

Major changes occurred in Britain's economy, politics, demography, education and national identity. In 1841 Britain dominated a global economic system. Its continued naval supremacy enabled the expansion of an empire of colonies. The country became the workshop of the world, following a coal-powered industrialisation. As a major exporter of manufactured goods and importer of raw materials, it locked other nations into dependant trading roles. This development ended just before the start of the final quarter of the nineteenth century with a worldwide recession, which lasted for over twenty years. The structure of the global economy reconfigured with new powers, foremost the United States and Germany, challenging Britain's position. What was regarded as free trade came to an end. The sometimes almost insatiable British thirst for labour was quenched, with growing concerns about poverty, depravation, overcrowding and labour conditions.

The role of the state in British society grew remarkably in terms of capacity and power. A new establishment came to trust the machinery of government, which – in their eyes – had helped to create a successful economy and disciplined groups who failed to support themselves or threatened the health and security of the wider population. In reality, despite reforms and new civil rights, the political elite tried to contain democratic aspirations of others or limit their influence. Electoral rights were only begrudgingly granted to increasing numbers of citizens. In 1884, about 30 per cent of the British population was enfranchised, but there was a growing working-class electorate. The major parties were the Whigs, and the more modern entities of Conservatives and Liberals, and they tended to supply the country with prime ministers. Numerous changes in power occurred. The Conservatives had already led governments before 1841. The Liberals first came to power in 1859. When the Liberals returned to government at the end of 1905, after 11 years in opposition, modern state control in social politics had begun to take shape. New solutions to the poverty problem were proposed and some were applied by a growing number of voluntary agencies, while social politics were implemented by the state through a system of welfare benefits.

The pressure for change also came from below. Workers went on strike to achieve better pay and working conditions. Unemployed workers set off on hunger marches. Labour formed a political party and trade union movement. However, social problems continued to cause disputes, and the labour unrest built up during the early twentieth century, affecting industries that were deemed vital to the economy and society as a whole. The army was deployed to subdue the unrest.

The underlying demographic changes were marked. Industrialisation caused greater movement of people across Britain, bringing them closer together from the countryside into the mushrooming cities. In particular, London grew, from 1801 doubling its size to almost three million inhabitants by 1861. As rural areas declined to the point of depopulation, the movement to the cities reached its peak at the end of the nineteenth century. In 1900, about 80 per cent of the total British population resided in urban conglomerates. People were living more closely together, the British population density doubled from 87 persons per square kilometre in 1841 to 180 in 1921. Furthermore, within the British cities and throughout the country, the population became more mobile through faster means of transport, notably the railways. Innovation in the means of communication also had an impact on daily life and could form a unifying force in social and national affairs.

Within this population resided a growing number of foreigners. From 1841 the census recorded their presence at 10-yearly intervals. These recordings are listed in Table 1.

The order in which the countries are listed underneath the all foreign-born total in Table 1 represents the largest numbers of foreign-born people per country in Britain in 1901 and 1911, the census years on either side of the Aliens Act of 1905. The Chinese, although forming a relatively small group,

Table 1. Census totals and selected countries of birth of foreign-born persons in Britain, 1841–1921

	1841	1851	1861	1871	1881	1891	1901	1911	1921
All foreign-born:									
– enumerated in England & Wales	39,244	61,708	101,832	139,445	174,372	233,008	339,436	373,516	311,185
– enumerated in Scotland	2,776	4,272	8,188	9,766	13,423	16,089	29,858	35,609	32,652
– total in Britain	42,020	65,980	110,020	149,211	187,795	249,097	369,294	409,125	343,837
– change per decennium on previous decennium		23,960	44,040	39,191	38,584	61,302	120,197	39,831	-65,288
Russia & Poland:									
– enumerated in England & Wales			5,249	9,569	14,468	45,074	82,844	95,541	103,040
– enumerated in Scotland			131	260	536	1,475	10,373	11,032	7,783
– total in Britain			5,380	9,829	15,004	46,549	93,217	106,573	110,823
Germany:									
– enumerated in England & Wales			28,644	32,823	37,301	50,599	49,133	53,324	22,128
– enumerated in Scotland			1,303	1,531	2,143	2,052	3,232	2,362	504
– total in Britain			29,947	34,354	39,444	52,651	52,365	55,686	22,632
France:									
– enumerated in England & Wales			12,989	17,876	14,596	20,797	20,467	28,827	33,486
– enumerated in Scotland			210	496	439	446	590	720	698
– total in Britain			13,199	18,372	15,035	21,243	21,057	29,547	34,184
Italy:									
– enumerated in England & Wales			4,489	5,063	6,504	9,909	20,332	20,389	20,957
– enumerated in Scotland			119	268	328	749	4,051	4,594	5,144
– Total in Britain			4,608	5,331	6,832	10,658	24,383	24,983	26,101
United States:									
– enumerated in England & Wales			7,861	8,270	17,767	19,740	16,668	13,637	37,045
– enumerated in Scotland					539	660	690	1,176	2,140
– total in Britain					18,306	20,400	17,358	14,813	39,185
China:									
– enumerated in England & Wales			146	199	202	767	387	1,319	4,382
– enumerated in Scotland					10	29	38	171	206
– total in Britain					212	796	425	1,490	4,588

have been included, because, as will be discussed, they became subject of brief but extraordinary intense public scrutiny.

The table shows an uneven process of immigration, with the highest influx of foreigners between 1881 and 1901, which partly coincided with the rapid growth of the total British population. In the decade before 1861, and again before 1891 and 1901, the foreign growth accelerated, but it slowed down after 1901 and the number of foreigners in Britain dropped before 1921. As part of the total population, the share of foreign-born people in Britain remained very small. Between 1841 and 1921 they made up less than 2 per cent of the entire population, apart from 1911 when it reached just over 2 per cent.[12] Only in a few cities and in specific areas in these cities did the settlement of foreigners extensively alter the composition of the population. The majority of the native Britons never met or was not in regular contact with foreigners. What they learned about immigrants came from sources such as newspapers.

Immigration was not a phenomenon that came into being in 1841; the census simply started to record the presence of foreigners. Much earlier influxes had occurred with the arrival of peoples such as the Saxons and Normans, groups such as Jews and Huguenots, and individuals such as traders, artists, musicians and craftsmen from Germany and Italy. During the middle period of the nineteenth century political refugees from continental Europe arrived. The increasing volume of migration into Britain during the second half of the nineteenth century was caused by economic developments, increased demand for labour and the open-door immigration policy in Britain, a global population explosion and the transport revolution, with the proliferation of trains and the advance of steamships enabling relatively fast and cheap travel.[13]

In addition to the groups listed in Table 1, as Panayi has calculated,[14] between 1815 and 1945 about one million Irish migrants came to Britain. They formed the vast majority of the total of about two and a half million immigrants that arrived here during this period. Some of them moved on and emigrated from Britain. Others settled down. The Irish arrival resulted in 1851 in a sizeable Irish-born population group in England and Wales. Another noticeable group among the immigrants was formed by about 220,000 Jews who came from Central and Eastern Europe.

The immigrants tended to settle in specific locations. According the 1901 census, 13 towns and cities in England and Wales contained a foreign-born population that amounted to more than 1 per cent of the town's or city's total population. The main three were London (under 3 per cent), Manchester and Tynemouth (both just over 2 per cent). The others were Cardiff, South Shields, Leeds, Grimsby, Kingston-upon-Hull, Liverpool, Bournemouth, Hornsby, Swansea and Willesden. In Scotland, cities like Glasgow, Edinburgh and Dundee had relatively high concentrations of immigrants. For example, in 1914 Glasgow contained the fourth largest Jewish population in Britain (about 7,000 persons, 0.9 per cent of the total population of the city). In 1901 almost half of the total foreign-born population of England and Wales resided in six London boroughs and three cities, namely Manchester, Liverpool and Leeds. This concentration, according to the census report, resulted in an exceptional situation in the London borough of Stepney, where a total population of about 298,600 contained some 54,000 foreigners, which according to the census report contributed to overcrowding, notably in the Stepney parish of Spitalfields that housed more than five times the London average number of people per acre. However, the foreign-born population of British cities, recorded in the census, did not consist entirely of residents, they included many men working on merchant navy ships that were anchored in the ports of these places.[15]

Despite being relatively small, the foreign presence and the perceived results of that presence were also related to expressions of feelings about national identity in a public debate, which was accommodated by growing literacy and new-style journalism.

Increased literacy came from rapidly developing education. In 1841 public schools, mostly private boarding institutions, taught the sons of wealthy families. Non-conformist churches and charity societies educated some of the poor, while the Church of England and the Scottish churches made a contribution through their Sunday schools. However, most people would probably still have failed a reading test if they were asked to take one, and mass education became a subject of public debate and eventually government policy. Ultimately, the Elementary Education Act was passed. It was the first of a number of acts between 1870 and 1893 that created compulsory education in England and Wales for all children aged between 5 and 13. The new law also established a system of school boards to build, manage and inspect free schools that were publicly funded. A separate act extended similar provisions to Scotland in 1872.

Compulsory elementary education enlarged literacy, which contributed to vast increases in the readership of British newspapers. At the start of the period under review the readership of daily newspapers largely consisted of well-educated individuals and persons with a prominent social, political and professional standing. The relatively high price of newspapers and the proportionately low literacy of the general public made papers comparatively inaccessible – some people borrowed them or depended on papers being read aloud by literate persons, for example, in public houses. However, lower prices came through the reduction of stamp duty on newspapers and its subsequent abolition as well as the repeal of paper duty, the availability of cheap printing paper and the application of more efficient printing presses. The advent of the railways eased the fast distribution of papers across wide areas. After 1870 more people learned to read. As children from working-class parents were educated, the attraction of reading newspapers rose. At the same time a growing electorate became interested in political news provided by the papers. Increasing numbers of women read newspapers. As the lighting of homes improved, people found it easier to peruse a paper in their spare time.

With their audiences, the papers changed too. Technical developments resulted in new fast rotation printing presses, which enabled further improvements in the quality of print and its contents. The telegraph allowed for faster and more extensive news collection; in 1909 the Empire Press Union was founded to transmit news across the globe. Newspaper style and subject matter were transformed. In 1842 the *Illustrated London News* was launched. Seven years later, it brought home the reality of the famine in Ireland in a series of weekly reports on the operation of the new poor law in an Irish county, creating sympathy with what was regarded in Britain as a poor sub-human race.[16] Half-tone photographs and new typefaces became part of innovative layouts and formats, such as the tabloid. In terms of contents, what also appealed to the widening readership were attractive advertisements and serial stories as well as interviews and coverage of popular and light-hearted or otherwise interesting subjects, such as crime.

New groups of readers often opted for new evening papers, which arose in the final quarter of the nineteenth century, both nationally in London and provincially or locally in other cities and towns. Whereas the traditional British press addressed and spoke for the establishment, the new papers, usually costing only a halfpenny, attempted to reach and speak for the working classes, notably white-collar workers and their families.

Using banner headlines, hot news, scandal stories and exciting competitions to grab the attention of potential readers and generate their interest, the new papers could evoke strong emotions. For example, military conflict had been a staple ingredient of the traditional newspapers, but through the new press the Second South African War (1899–1902) entered the kitchens and living rooms of many ordinary families. Of course, family members corresponded with husbands, fathers, sons, uncles and nephews serving in South Africa, but the popular papers had a huge impact on people's knowledge of the war and helped to determine their attitude towards the conflict, which they expressed in letters sent to editors that were published next to detailed and illustrated reports from knowledgeable war correspondents.

This did not mean that these newspapers invariably told their readers what they wanted to hear. Early in the Second South African War, one of the papers, the *Daily Mail*, pointed out the seriousness of the situation; from the outset of the hostilities it argued that no fewer than a hundred thousand well-equipped men would be needed to subdue the Boer enemy. This independent view led to a head-on collision with the government, which decided to cut the paper off from all War Office news. However, journalists from other papers rallied to its cause and handed news to Sarah Wilson, the first female war correspondent who worked for the *Daily Mail*. The conflict did the paper no harm. Its circulation rose by 300,000 copies in March 1900 when it published the story of the first British successes in South Africa.

Thus, the nature of journalism changed. By and large, the papers combined objectivity in news reporting with an opinionated editorial perspective, not just to express popular feelings, inform and convince the public, and influence parliament and government, but also to create a faithful readership that was concerned about the issues championed by the papers.

Finally, the experience of national identity changed. Throughout the period 1841–1921, common identities could be defined with multiple, often overlapping specifications. For example, identity could be linked or expressed along national lines such as British, English, Welsh, Irish and Scottish. Regional and local characteristics also gave identity colour, as did tribal, clan and family attributes. British army life, experienced by professional soldiers, volunteers and their families or felt through association by the general public, was another powerful source of identity. The Royal House and loyalty to the Crown contributed to British identity, notably under the long reign of Queen Victoria,[17] and by 1914 allegiance to the empire had come to the fore.

Tradition also played a major role in identity, similar to shared beliefs about what were regarded as essential and eternal religious, intellectual and moral truths, norms and values. However, people were also divided, for example, along religious lines, and battered by constant change, and as economic crises arose and the contrast between rich and poor in the cities sharpened, feelings of unrest were accompanied by rising doubts about old beliefs. And while some sought to adapt, others resisted change. Nevertheless, it seemed as if authority based on convention began to crumble. Towards the end of the nineteenth century the British establishment started to question its domination. Class divisions were accentuated and gender distinctions became distinct. Sometimes people found it difficult to define their own identity, but it was always possible to state that they were unlike other people, such as foreigners in general or immigrants in particular, often based on bias against those who looked or acted differently.

The new identity contained chauvinism: the national needs transcended all needs; and other nations were often resented.[18] In the experience of identity, the concept of race became a powerful indicator.[19] In 1883 Francis Galton introduced his ideas on eugenics, one of many theories on inherited or mutated characteristics, such as Social Darwinism. Eugenics expressed the idea that not the circumstances in which people grew up but inborn ethnic factors determined their physical and mental traits such as intelligence, work ethic and susceptibility to criminal behaviour. It was part of a set of beliefs that promoted improving the genetic quality of a human population by excluding genetic groups judged to be less desirable, and favouring genetic groups judged to be superior.

These eugenic ideas were applied to news about colonial revolts, Irish home rule campaigns and rising immigration – hardening attitudes about perceived racial differences. They were also extended to the metropolitan poor, feeding on concerns about the stagnation of national growth and degeneration of public health. In this atmosphere of anxiety, it was as if the British, English or Scottish population stocks were diluted with unfit and feeble foreigners. Just as the influx of Irish migrants after the famine was said to have threatened English and Scottish prosperity, the immigrant incursion was reported to increase poverty, depravation, overcrowding, insanitary conditions and disease that threatened the health of the nation. The *Daily Mail* argued that increased immigration 'followed by a steady decline in the British birth-rate' created a parasite population with crime, misery and destitution that 'weakens the growth and reproduction force of the people on which it battens. The higher standard of life yields slowly but certainly before the lower, as the oak is first exhausted and then killed by the mistletoe which preys upon its sap.'[20] Such ideas got a sexual edge in August Forel's *Die sexualle Frage* (1903), which degraded black people and Jews. The book was translated into English and read in Britain.

As these ideas about race emerged, the Second South African War proved to be a watershed moment. There had already been a series of military conflicts in the area now known as South Africa. Although ultimately victorious, on occasion the British armies appeared exposed – disproving the British self-belief of invulnerability.[21] In 1878 the British suffered a defeat at Isandlwana at the hands of the Zulus.[22] During the First South African War, when the United Kingdom fought the South African or Transvaal Republic, which had declared independence, the British army was defeated at Majuba Hill in 1881. These were not the only setbacks on this continent. Four years later, in another part of Africa, Charles Gordon – previously commander of the 'Ever Victorious Army' in China – was killed in the Sudan during his unsuccessful defence of Khartoum against the Mahdi army.

The self-doubt came to a head in the Second South African War, when Britain and English-speaking settlers in the Cape and Natal Colonies fought the Afrikaans-speaking Boers, who had two independent republics in South Africa – the Transvaal Republic and the Orange Free State. At first, the Afrikaners outnumbered the British soldiers three to one, and they besieged the imperial army at Ladysmith, Mafeking and Kimberley. The outlook for Britain was bleak and the view that it would lose the war was widespread.[23] What followed in Britain was a wave of jingoism and a rush to recruit volunteers, and the British eventually defeated their opponents.

While the earlier defeats in Africa caused anguish, which eroded the British self-confidence but did not produce fundamental disquiet,[24] the Second South African War heightened the feeling of crisis, notably when the public learned from newspaper reports that military doctors had deemed three out of every five British men who volunteered for military duty in South Africa as physically unfit to serve. This stoked feelings about the dangers to what was regarded as the white Anglo-Saxon race, which was deemed being threatened or diluted by immigration of foreigners.

Sources

To study changing attitudes and language use against the background described above, this book critically examines primary sources, which for this purpose have so far been somewhat underused. A selection of dictionaries and the *Historical Thesaurus of English* are consulted to establish the various definitions, meanings and applications of the word alien and to determine whether they changed during this period. These definitions, senses and uses are employed in quantitative and qualitative analyses of the occurrence of the word alien in a selection of British newspapers, published between 1841 and 1921. In the quantitative analysis the newspapers are examined within a context of other British English publications from that period. A small number of publicly accessible digital collections of these publications is selected, because it is practically impossible in this relatively small book to examine the entire publication output of the period. The selection contains printed census reports and corpora of British English books, parliamentary debate records, pamphlets and newspapers. The chosen collections thus offer an impression of word choice in which the relevance of language use in newspapers can be established.

The analyses in this book pay attention to a selection of national, regional and local newspapers from across Britain. As highlighted above, during the period under review newspapers played a large, yet limited role in circulating news, forming opinion and voicing views. In addition, books and pamphlets were published, but like the papers they were not read universally, although with growing literacy their readership grew enormously during the last three decennia of the period under review. News and opinions also spread by word-of-mouth – on the street, in the workplace and at home. Incidental gatherings too gave people a chance to hear news and exchange views, for example, during sport matches, concerts and music hall events, and organised meetings in schools, churches, women's suffrage groups, working men's clubs and temperance societies. In the twentieth century cinemas with newsreels and moving pictures started gaining ground, but the new picture houses did not always charge admission prices that everybody could afford and thus only played a restricted role before 1921. Within the scope of this book it is unfeasible to review all the media that determined and expressed people's attitudes, and therefore a decision has been made to concentrate on a cross-section of the British press, consisting of five newspapers.

From the national daily newspapers that appeared throughout the period between 1841 and 1921 and are available in a digital format suitable for searches and analyses, *The Times* has been chosen. Published in London, it was one of Britain's oldest and most influential papers, building and voicing public opinion. By 1841, the foundation of its position as Britain's pre-eminent national journal had been laid. From 1803, under publisher John Walter II and from 1817 editor Thomas Barnes, *The Times* had developed into a strong daily, which was widely respected for its foreign news and national coverage, where it had a lasting impact on the views of many Britons. Its daily circulation of about 40,000 in 1851 rose to about 65,000 in 1861.[25] In an average month, such as June 1845, the paper usually had 12 pages, rising to 16 in 1865 and 20 in 1875, after which the regular daily number of pages fluctuated between 16 and 20.[26] Although its editorial views were independent, *The Times* can be seen as a champion of the middle classes, interpreter of public opinion and epitome of the British establishment, notably the Liberals.

The second selected daily newspaper is the *London Evening Standard*, which began publishing in 1827 as *The Standard*, founded by businessman Charles Baldwin and its first editor Stanley Lees Giffard. By 1860 it had two editions, with a joint total circulation of up to 46,000 in 1861 – *The Standard* came out in the morning, followed later in the day by *The Evening Standard*, since 1857 the oldest British evening newspaper, which eventually became the paper's only edition. By the mid-1880s its circulation was about 250,000. After 1899 it declined, with a 1904 circulation of about 80,000. The paper was renowned for its foreign news coverage. It was one of the principal Conservative papers.[27]

The third paper is the *Daily Mail*, the outspoken member of the new popular press that rose to prominence in Britain towards the end of the nineteenth century. It was first published in 1896, more concise in its coverage than *The Times* and the *London Evening Standard*, and it had a print-run on the first day of almost 400,000, which rose to about 600,000 in 1899. By 1900 its circulation peaked at 989,255. It was founded by Alfred Harmsworth, later Lord Northcliffe, who worked closely with his brother Harold, later Lord Rothermere. The *Daily Mail* presented itself as 'the busy man's paper', but it was derided by Prime Minister Lord Salisbury (Robert Cecil) as 'a newspaper produced by office boys for office boys'.[28] It did not always please the public and had a habit of upsetting the authorities, but the paper was partisan, patriotic and supported British imperialism. It has been labelled the 'Voice of Empire in London journalism'.[29]

To counter the bias towards England and the London-based newspapers, the fourth selected paper is the *Glasgow Herald*, which started in 1783 as the *Glasgow Advertiser*, but changed its name in 1802. By 1850 the paper had become the leading daily in the west of Scotland, under owner George Outram, with a circulation of about 4,500 in 1855, but within a decade it was printing about 25,000 copies. By that time the paper reported and commented on Scottish and local affairs, but it also made space for international and national news. The *Glasgow Herald* can be seen as a Tory mouthpiece until 1836, thereafter it drifted into a mildly Whiggish direction. It continued to be moderately Liberal and after 1886 became an advocate of Liberal Unionism.[30]

To supply a sample of one of the new papers with a local focus and complete the cross-section of the British press, a paper from Nottingham has been chosen. On the eve of the First World War Nottingham had about 260,000 inhabitants. It was a medium-sized city, smaller than London, Glasgow, Manchester, Birmingham, Liverpool, Leeds and Sheffield, almost on par with Hull and Bradford, and larger than Leicester, Derby, Coventry and Stoke-on-Trent.[31] One of the city's main papers was the *Nottingham Evening Post*. No estimated circulation figures are available. It was founded in 1878 by Thomas Forman – the first evening paper in Nottingham – and from 1902 the paper published daily editions, claiming religious and political independence.[32]

These five newspapers sometimes offer only an impressionistic view, but together they do provide a valuable resource on attitudes towards immigrants and use of the word alien.

Methodology

The selected newspaper sources are examined in a quantitative and a qualitative analysis of the use of the word alien. To make these analyses feasible, publicly accessible digital collections have been searched to produce statistical datasets. These collections contain papers of which the contents have been captured using optical character recognition software. Unfortunately, at present this technology still causes imprecision, which can also result from the manner of data gathering, digitisation processes and differences in the available search programmes – different deposits, available through the British Newspaper Archive, British Library and Gale Historical Newspapers, use different software and search methods.³³ Search results also vary, depending on the use of different search criteria, such as exact terms and phrases, quotation marks or logical (or Boolean) operators, proximity operators and wildcards. Furthermore, the size of some of the collections, such as the British Newspaper Archive, is still growing with the addition of newspapers, while the technology is further developed to overcome inaccuracy.

As a result, the statistical datasets that are produced here through searches contain errors or remain incomplete. For example, a search for the word alien also brings up many misspellings and words the reading programme recognises as alien but are not actually alien, such as Allen or Allan. In contrast, even a precise or exact search – when possible – does not guarantee that all instances in which alien was used are found. Furthermore, digital entries could have been erroneously duplicated, which means an occurrence is counted more than once, or some entries have multiple uses of the word alien but are counted as one.³⁴ In contrast, entire articles or pages are occasionally missing from a digital file, while for some years the records of some papers are missing or the data are reported as unreliable. Finally, identical searches in one collection but spread over a period of time can provide different results because the collection has been extended between the searches.

At the time of writing this book large academic research projects, for example, in Lancaster and Bristol, are creating new corpora that contain newspapers, and they are applying technology that potentially eliminates errors, but this technology was unavailable to the author of this book. To overcome this obstacle, the analysis in this book is based on multiple checks of a relevant digital newspaper record that is available through the British Newspaper Archive, British Library and Gale Historical Newspapers, including basic and advanced searches, with the results being merged into a single outcome.

In general, data collection and replication are of course also sensitive to error. Statistical fluctuation can appear to be random or caused by variants that are too small to be detected.³⁵ Therefore, the quantitative search results in this book probably contain more than the usual statistical mistakes, and their value is not in providing exact and comprehensive numbers, but in revealing trends in word use.

The checks of the digital newspaper records are accompanied by an application of critical methods in the qualitative analysis to examine a record, its context and the events and people mentioned or implied in the text. This enables the selection of particular information from newspaper articles and the synthesis of these particulars into a chronologically ordered narrative in the qualitative analysis.

Working this way and taking all the shortcomings into account, the linguistic historical approach applied in this book brings out how attitudes to immigrants in Britain changed between 1841 and 1921 and what language was used to put these changing attitudes into words, in particular the word alien, with its specific meanings, the overtones it bore and what people meant or felt when they used it.

Chapter 1

THE MEANINGS OF ALIEN

The *Oxford English Dictionary* (*OED*)[1] records the first English use of the word alien in 1382, when the Wycliffite Bible translation mentioned an 'alyen godde'. It is noted again by the *OED* in 1387, referring to an 'alien lord'. In this sense the adjective alien came to mean belonging to another person, place or family, not of one's own, or from elsewhere and foreign. More specifically, in relation to a person, it adopted the sense of having been born in or owing allegiance to a foreign country, especially designating a foreigner who is not a naturalised citizen of the country where they are situated. 'Alien' acquired several connotations: of a foreign nature or character; strange, unfamiliar and different; and hostile and repugnant.

The *OED* is one of the main historical dictionaries of English. It traces the development of that language and provides a comprehensive reference guide. However, compilation of the dictionary did not begin until 1857, after the start of the period under review, 1841–1921, and it was not until 1884 that it was published as an ongoing project in separate instalments. Thus, the *OED* did not exist at the start of the reviewed period and its producers could have been influenced by anachronism and other factors at the time of their compilation, such as academic bias, which determined their choice or emphasis of word meanings.[2] Therefore, the *Historical Thesaurus of English*[3] better illustrates what the word alien meant for people during the entire period under review and what alternatives for this term were available to contemporary users of the language. The *Historical Thesaurus* charts the development of meaning in the vocabulary of English. It consists of recorded words from Anglo-Saxon times to the present day.

Noun

Alien appears in the *Historical Thesaurus* as a noun, adjective and verb. As a noun, it belongs to several categories, notably the subcategory 'stranger and outsider'. This contains a few dozen words, which had similar meanings, and it indicates when records of their use were found. Apart from alien, recorded from 1330 to the present, words with the same meaning and relevant to the period 1841–1921 include stranger, from ca. 1385 to the present; barbarian, between 1549 and 1862; outsider, from 1800; and foreigner, between 1565 and 1700 and from 1855 to the present. Also included, but nowadays unfamiliar: inconnu(e), from 1807; outrigger, noted in 1852; offcome, noted in 1859; and offcomer, from 1898. Although foreigner is not recorded in this subcategory between 1700 and 1855, it appears in the subcategories 'an incomer and visitor' and 'from another country', respectively from 1421 and 1413 to the present. This suggests that, while from 1855 foreigner also had the meanings of stranger and outsider, it was used with various meanings throughout the period 1841–1921.

These entries indicate that between 1841 and 1921 the main alternatives for the word alien were stranger, outsider and foreigner. This book largely follows the *OED* and defines a stranger as a person from another place, town or country. An outsider is regarded here as a person who does not belong to a specific group or community. A foreigner is a person born in or belonging to another country.

The noun alien can also denote a specific type of inhabitant, that is, a non-native one. As such, it was recorded by the *Historical Thesaurus* from 1330. Nouns with a similar denotation include: stranger, from 1375; out-comeling, between 1400 and 1555; free-denizen, between 1576 and 1653; and denizen, from 1576.

Nouns in the subcategory 'stranger and outsider' that were older than alien, often coming from Old English and being of Germanic or Scandinavian origin, but with one exception (fremd) not noted during the period under review, include: guest (giest), recorded until 1578; fremd (fremda), recorded until 1580, but also noted in 1871 (similar to fremman (1568–1639) and frenne (1579–1614)); and the Scots word farandman, recorded from ca. 1205 until 1609. Later words, but no longer relevant in 1841 are out-comeling, after 1400 until 1555; and estranger, between 1471 and 1641 and between 1721 and 1800.

This historical use of the noun alien is confirmed by the *OED*, which states that an alien is a person who does not belong to a particular family, community or country – a foreigner, stranger or outsider. More specifically, it states that an alien is a foreigner who is not a naturalised citizen of the country where they are living, a foreign national. In a religious context, it can also be a person who is separated or excluded from a particular community. Since 1580, an alien could furthermore be a person who is opposed, repugnant or unaccustomed, or a stranger to a specified someone or something.

The use of alien in English, meaning a foreigner who is not a naturalised citizen of the country where they are living, and the idea of a foreign national in general are related to the development of nation states, characterised by a shared ethnicity and citizenship, which started in Western Europe in the fifteenth century but did not become a European-wide phenomenon until the nineteenth century.[4] The *Historical Thesaurus* has recorded the use of nation from about 1300: in the sense of a country from ca. 1320; and meaning a state from 1568. However, nationality – the characteristics of a national of a country – is more recent, recorded from 1828. It is related to the older word citizenship – that is, the rights of a citizen of a town or city, recorded from 1611; or the status of an inhabitant of a country, different to that of a foreigner, recorded from 1831.

Foreigners in Britain who did not have British citizenship or nationality included refugees and immigrants, and as such these words could also be used as alternatives for alien. The use of refugee, in the sense of an exile or stateless person, is recorded by the *Historical Thesaurus* from 1685. Immigrant is recorded from 1792. This book, again broadly following the *OED*, defines a refugee as a person driven from their home by persecution, war or other causes to seek refuge elsewhere, notably in another country. An immigrant is a person who settles as a resident in another country than the one they were born in.

Adjective

As an adjective, meaning strange or foreign, alien is recorded in the *Historical Thesaurus* from 1340. Meaning of a foreign nation or allegiance, it is noted from 1450. In the sense of non-native, alien is recorded by the *Historical Thesaurus* from 1450. Adjectives at the same level include: transregionate, only recorded in 1577; overun, in 1881 and 1886; and non-patrial, from 1971 to the present. However, alien could also be used as an adjective meaning different, distinct and directly opposed to. As such, it is recorded in the *Historical Thesaurus* from 1382. Words relevant for the period 1841–1921 at the same level of alien in the sense of different and distinct include: discriminate, recorded from 1626 to 1887; discriminated, from 1783 to 1848; and well-marked from 1797. In the sense of directly opposed to: repugnant from 1387 or 1388 to 1864; oppugnant, from 1513; contrariant, from 1530 to 1842; and obverse, recorded in 1840.

Other uses

Alien had other uses. In the years between 1841 and 1921 it could also be applied as: a verb, to mean to quarrel (until 1870); a legal term for a specific action, meaning the transfer of property; a botanical term, meaning of foreign growth or origin; and a linguistic term, meaning borrowed from another language. However, it appears that as such, alien was mainly used by specialists in legal or scholarly discourse, not in everyday language.

It was not until well after 1921 that alien developed a new significance, referring to a being from another planet or an extraterrestrial. The *OED* traces this sense to a 1931 issue of the American science-fiction magazine *Wonder Stories*, which apparently first presented such a creature.

Samuel Johnson

Further evidence of the availability for use of the word alien in 1841 can be found in Samuel Johnson's *Dictionary of the English Language*.[5] This work was published from 1755 and new editions were available in 1841. It used citations, which provide a context and an insight into the connotations of words for contemporaries.

In the first two editions of his *Dictionary*, Johnson listed an alien as a foreigner, a person from another country of family. He gave several citations, including quotations from Shakespeare's work such as *The Merchant of Venice*:

> If it be prov'd against an alien,
> He seeks the life of any citizen,
> The party, 'gainst the which he doth contrive,
> Shall seize on half their goods.

This is followed by a quote from John Davies (1569–1626), an English poet, lawyer and politician who sat in the House of Commons and became Attorney General for Ireland: 'The mere Irish were not only accounted aliens, but enemies, and altogether out of the protection of the law; so as it was no capital offence to kill them.' And the words from Joseph Addison (1672–1719), an English essayist, poet, playwright and politician: 'Their famous lawgiver condemned the persons, who sat idle in divisions dangerous to the government, as aliens to the community, and therefore to be cut off from it.'

Johnson also referred to the legal concept of an alien: 'one born in a strange country, and never enfranchised' and narrowed it by omitting persons born abroad from English parents. And he listed the word as an adjective: foreign, or not of the same family or land; and estranged from. In addition, Johnson defined the verb to alien: to make anything the property of another; and to estrange, to turn the mind or affection or to make averse to.[6]

Modern dictionaries

Like the *OED*, modern dictionaries emphasise the legal concept highlighted by Johnson and sometimes accentuate a slightly different negative connotation of an alien, namely not just an enemy or outsider, but also an unfamiliar, unlikeable, strange and frightening person.

The *Merriam-Webster Dictionary* defines alien relatively neutrally as follows: (1a) belonging or relating to another person, place, or thing (strange, an alien environment); (b) relating, belonging or owing allegiance to another country or government (foreign, alien residents); (c) exotic (alien plants); (d) coming from another world (extraterrestrial alien beings, an alien spaceship); and (2) differing in nature or character typically to the point of incompatibility (ideas alien to democracy).[7]

In *Collins English Dictionary* alien means: (1) belonging to a different country, race or group, usually one you do not like or are frightened of; (2) something that seems strange and perhaps frightening, because it is not part of your normal experience; (3) something different from normal feelings or behaviour; (4) someone who is not a legal citizen of the country in which they live; and (5) a creature from outer space.[8]

Finally, the *Cambridge Dictionary* offers (1) coming from a different country, race, or group; (2) strange and not familiar; (3) relating to creatures from another planet; and (4) (in law) someone who lives in a country of which they are not a legal citizen.[9]

Legal concept

According to the *OED*, alien as an adjective and noun was borrowed from Latin and French, following *alienus* (belonging to another) and *alius* (other).[10] However, in the sense of an alien being a foreigner, stranger or non-native, the etymon was evidently taken from these languages, but linguistic evolution in different countries produced divergence. In Western Europe a specific word with the meaning of an alien being a foreigner who is not a naturalised citizen of the country where they are living does not seem to exist in non-English languages. Instead of an alien, present-day French uses *étranger(ère)*, somebody from abroad. Spanish has *extranjero (extranjera)*, meaning a foreigner. Italian employs *straniero(-a)*, a stranger, and *forestiero(-a)*, which means of a foreign country. In comparison, Germans say *Ausländer(in)*, and talk about people or things being *fremd* or *fremdländisch*, which means strange or from a foreign country.[11]

Perhaps part of this language evolution in Britain was related to developments in English and Scottish law, which eventually created a legal concept of an alien being a person in the United Kingdom who is not a national or citizen of the United Kingdom. According to the *OED*, this notion had already taken shape in a 1433 order of the Privy Council, which had the force of law, using the term aliens in a decree on the merchandise on ships.[12] There are earlier references. One of them dated from the fourteenth century and reappeared in a report on a murder trial in 1849 in *The Times*,[13] which will be discussed later. One of the defendants was said to have been an alien, and an extensive discussion took place about an alien statute from Edward III (1312–1377). The fourteenth-century legislation reportedly gave aliens the right to be tried *per medietatum lingue* – by a jury *de medietate lingue*, that is, a jury containing aliens.[14]

Legislation, specifically aimed at aliens, further developed in 1703 with the Scottish Act of Security, which in itself was a response to the 1701 English Act of Settlement that enabled the Hanover Succession (reserving the English and Irish crowns for Protestants – the next Protestant in line to the throne was Sophia of Hanover). The Scottish law intended to place Scotland on an even footing with England in the negotiations about the new shared sovereign. The English replied with the 1705 Alien Act, which threatened to treat all non-domiciled Scots in England as foreigners. The conflict came to an end with the 1707 Acts of Union, which created the United Kingdom, and was followed by the 1709 General Naturalisation Act. In 1772 Parliament passed the British Nationality Act, which sought to formulate who belonged to the nation.

The concept of an alien was included in the *Commentaries on the Laws of England* by William Blackstone, published from 1765 in Oxford, and in *The Law Dictionary*, compiled by Thomas Edlyne and Giles Jacob, published in 1809 in London. These works were regarded as influential treatises on the common law of England and used as reference works for judicial decisions, which relied on precedent rather than statute.[15]

The development took a new turn with the 1793 Aliens Act, with 'regulations respecting aliens arriving in this kingdom, or resident therein'.[16] This law was an attempt to register but not restrict immigration of foreigners. Aliens were ordered to give personal details, for example, their name, occupation and address. The information was noted by a local Justice of the Peace and eventually forwarded to the Aliens Office in London. Subsequently, new laws were passed, including the 1798 Act for Establishing Regulations Respecting Aliens, or acts were renewed, as in 1806, 1816 and 1826. In 1836, the Registration of Aliens Act repealed previous alien legislation.

The 1836 law[17] enabled the cataloguing of aliens, not their expulsion, unlike the Aliens Removal Act, passed by the British parliament in 1848,[18] due to be in force for one year, renewable thereafter but repealed in 1850. Despite other legislation, such as naturalisation or extradition acts, for more than 50 years no further laws were adopted to regulate the general presence of aliens in Britain. During this half century and different from other countries, there was no legislation on immigration. Therefore, the United Kingdom had no means of excluding a foreigner who wished to enter. The only remaining provision was an act from the reign of William IV (1830–1837), which required the master of a ship arriving in Britain to declare the number of aliens on board to the chief customs officer in the port of arrival. In 1892, and again in 1894 and 1898, bills on aliens were announced. However, they were not passed into law. The 1904 Aliens Bill met a similar fate, being abandoned at the committee stage. In contrast, the 1905 Aliens Bill was passed and came into force in 1906.

The 1905 Aliens Act sought to restrict immigration but was limited to steerage (not cabin) passengers on ships arriving at specified British ports. It did not apply to transmigrants, people who passed through Britain on their way to other destinations. Immigrants who were refused entry had the right of appeal. The Act formulated the right of asylum for refugees, for example, mentioning people who were fleeing religious persecution abroad. Entry into the kingdom could be denied for several reasons, for instance, when the arrivals appeared to lack sufficient means of subsistence, were found in unsanitary condition or had been judged to be unhealthy or insane. With regard to aliens who had been successful entrants and thus living in Britain, the home secretary could seek court approval to expel convicted alien criminals and aliens who had become dependent on poor relief. An unsuccessful attempt to modify this law in 1911 was the Aliens (Prevention of Crime) Bill.

The 1914 Aliens Restriction Act curtailed immigration and eased the deportation of resident aliens. It was accompanied by the 1914 British Nationality and Status of Aliens Act, which defined who was a British national or subject on the basis of a person's place of birth or status of naturalisation – a foreigner in Britain was admitted to the citizenship when after an application this person was found to be of good character, possessed adequate knowledge of the English language, swore an oath of allegiance and paid a standard fee. The 1914 Act was superseded by the 1918 British Nationality and Status of Aliens Act, the 1919 Aliens Act and the 1919 Aliens Restriction (Amendment) Act, with subsequent regulations such as the 1920 Aliens Order imposing stronger official controls on immigration.[19]

During the twentieth century further UK legislation was put into place, for example, in 1948, 1962, 1968 and 1971, with, as Davies has written, the 1981 British Nationality Act for the first time putting British citizenship onto the statute book, and defining a British citizen as a person who had the right of entry to the United Kingdom.[20] However, others had this right too – Irish citizens possessed it, as did EU citizens from 1991 to 2020, and in 1998 it was extended to residents of the kingdom's remaining Overseas Territories.

This brief legal history shows that before 1921 occasionally – in particular between 1793 and 1815, in 1848 and between 1914 and 1919 – the Westminster parliament passed specific alien laws, notably at times of war and revolutionary crisis. It has not explained the attempts from 1892, resulting in the 1905 Aliens Act, but these ventures and their background will be discussed later. As a clear, consistent and authorised definition of British citizenship was not formulated until much later in the twentieth century, it has to be assumed that a rather fluent legal concept of who was an alien was established in Britain before 1841 and used throughout the period to 1921.

Language change

The meanings of alien developed in a language that was changing. Contemporaries were aware of these changes, which were not always welcomed. In a leading article on the use of English, *The Times* wrote in 1910: 'Language usually expresses men's feeling about a thing',[21] and a year later the editor hoped for the 'preservation of our mother tongue from corruption'. As an example of that misuse, he mentioned the word racial. Derived from race, not a word of Latin origin, it could not be 'racial', and instead 'ethnic' should be used – like local, from place, not placial. The article joked: 'But "racial", though an undesirable alien at the outset, is now perhaps a naturalized citizen of the language.'[22]

During the period under review, English was – as it nowadays still is – a living language and therefore in a constant state of flux.[23] In general, language change can be triggered by different forces and occur for many reasons. For example, events and developments in the wider society can instigate and facilitate language change. Living languages also maintain an internal dynamic, and changes in a language can be derived from that dynamic. Change often concerns words, which can describe tangible objects, emotions and abstract concepts. In terms of their meaning, words can take on meanings that are associated with specific domains of their use. When the use of a word changes, its meaning can change too. For example, when the use changes from specialised to everyday situations. Many words thus accrue layers of different meaning in a widening range of contexts, the more so when they are applied in various types of communication. While some words fall out of use (and are sometimes revived later), new words enter the language, coming in when people grow aware of the object they describe.

Language change can also be brought about by users of a language coming in contact with users of other languages. This contact can be instrumental for increasing the word stock of a language; new words are relatively easily added, more so than grammatical forms and structures. Borrowing or copying from other languages is a way of sourcing new words. The words alien, foreigner, stranger and non-native were all borrowed from Latin and French, and immigrant was also of Latin origin.[24] However, borrowing can affect the meaning of a word as its new users may select connotations of that word, give it a different status, attach prestige or shame, or alter the meaning altogether.[25]

Linguists distinguish different types of meaning. Leith has listed six, which are applied here: conceptual, in mentioning or alluding to something; connotative, on how something is perceived; stylistic, on a particular context of the use of something; affective, on how people feel about something in terms of attitude and evaluation, or concerning class, race or other emblems (including abusive symbols); reflected, when a word has more than one associated meaning; and collocative, when a meaning is derived from a juxtaposition or association of the word.[26] One word can have one or more of these types of meaning.

There are different kinds of semantic change. Words can be manipulated by language users as they are handed down through generations, which can emphasise or alter one of more types of meaning. And – a regular phenomenon in language change – old words can get new meanings. Such changes go through stages. For example, a conceptual meaning can be acquired and then changed or dropped.

Common changes of meaning are extension, degeneration and restriction. The opposite processes are narrowing, regeneration and generalisation. In extension, the meaning is widened. In degeneration, an extension appears to so many senses of a meaning that a particular meaning is lost. In restriction, the meaning is reduced to less than it originally conveyed.[27] An example of extension is the word dean, formerly meaning head of a chapter in a cathedral church, but now used as a designation for the senior or foremost person of any group, like a dean of sportswriters. An example of regeneration is the word sturdy which moved from disparagement in the sense of harsh, rough or intractable to strong in present-day speech. Meanings can of course also be transferred from one word to another.

These changes are sometimes caused by shifts in attitudes and social values. In terms of connotative and affective meaning, standard changes caused by shifts in attitudes and values are: amelioration, that is the elevation of meaning; and pejoration, the degradation of meaning. For instance, the change of a meaning can be an amelioration, where a word's affective meaning moves from disapproval to favourable. An example is the word nice, which first meant foolish, simple, ignorant, senseless or absurd, but now is pleasant or attractive. An example of pejoration is 'silly', originally denoting happy, blissful, blessed or fortunate, it became senseless, absurd or foolish. Pejoration can occur in words that describe groups of people, and some of these words can carry a social stigma.[28] As the word alien appears in modern dictionaries with negative connotations of being hostile, unlikeable and frightening, which it did not have when Johnson compiled his dictionary, its meaning must have been degraded as the English language developed.

English before 1841

The development of the English language can be divided into four periods: Old English, before ca. 1100; Middle English, from ca. 1100 to ca. 1500; Early Modern English, from ca. 1500 to ca. 1800; and Modern English, from ca. 1800 to the present. During the Old English period, the language developed from an Indo-European to a Germanic language. During the fifth and sixth centuries[29] it was spoken alongside and also influenced by the languages of Roman Britain – Brittonic and Late Spoken Latin, but these languages were eventually dominated by Old English. Its vocabulary was mostly native Germanic, with borrowed words from Greek, Latin and Scandinavian languages.

While the Roman period and the arrival of Christianity had resulted in significant additions from Latin to the English vocabulary, borrowing words from Latin and French was the principal means of word stock expansion in the Middle English period. The main cause of borrowing was the Norman conquest, after which 'alien' was adopted – the introduction of the word in the English vocabulary has been placed by the *Chronological English Dictionary*[30] between 1150 and 1450, coming from Old French.

The reasons for borrowing 'alien' remain unclear. The motivation for adopting French words in general varied during the Middle English period. They were sometimes needed in specific texts or for special religious, scientific, legal and literary purposes. Occasionally they were borrowed to provide stylistic resonance, because of their formal and official sound. Perhaps 'alien' was borrowed for official documents because it denoted a legal status or resonated thoughts about groups of people.

However, during the thirteenth century the incursion of the French into British society also aroused hostility, and this wakened a consciousness of differences, in which the knowledge of English came to be regarded as a proper mark of Englishness. That may have hampered the wider application of words such as alien. In response, as the language entered the Early Modern English period, scholars put up a defence of borrowing, with adaptation and reintroduction, sometimes creating new meanings and interpretations. The medieval belief in the superiority of Latin survived long after 1500. It remained the language of power and prestige, subject of wholesale borrowing, contributing to a vocabulary of learned words of Latin and French origin, next to a body of everyday words, mainly Germanic in origin. The Germanic words often had strong connotative or affective meanings, and the words of Latin and French origin tended to be more neutral, referred to abstract concepts and were applied in more formal writing.

Meanwhile, language use was affected by another process – standardisation. English knew, and still knows, an assortment of regional, local and sectional varieties. What eventually became the standard British English variety emerged ca. 1400, influenced by the East Midlands variety, which was spoken by merchants in London. It was subsequently assimilated by others, either deliberately or involuntary, so that a process of standardisation occurred throughout Britain. This process was not the outcome of an official policy but was forced and encouraged by cultural institutions and individuals, mostly based in London, and emulated by organisations and persons in Edinburgh and Dublin.

Leith and Graddol[31] have distinguished four sociolinguistic processes in standardisation, and their model is adopted for this book: selection, choosing a variant; elaboration, ensuring it can be used for wide range of functions; codification, reducing its variability; and implementation, making texts available and encouraging users to adopt the standard variety. Elaboration started when English was selected for use in administrative and legal courts. From the sixteenth century, codification of English was conducted by a small elite of scholars, including Johnson, who fixed the spelling of words and prescribed the grammar. Through early standardisation 'alien' received its modern spelling and conceptual meanings.

Codification coincided with the export of the English language, mostly to areas of the United Kingdom within the British Isles such as Wales, Scotland and Ireland, and to the colonies and territories of the British Empire. Eventually this created different linguistic varieties, such as British, American and Australian English, which all contained the word alien, unlike Afrikaans, the Germanic language of the Boers in South Africa, who used the noun 'uitlander'.

British English

Throughout the period 1841–1921 the semantic content of many British English words shifted and new words came in. As stated earlier, *The Times* wrote about these changes. In 1910 it observed: 'Nowadays people like their new words to be as artificial as possible. [...] Afterwards, when the novelty of the thing has worn off, they often seem to grow tired of the length and artificiality of the word, and perhaps devise some shorter or simpler substitute for it.'[32] Examples were aviators and aeronauts, which became airmen (like seamen); telegram, which changed to wire; automobile, which turned to motor; and cinematoscope, which was shortened to cinema. A year later, the paper deplored the changing meaning of mutual, which was increasingly used as synonym for common (as in shared), and of phenomenal, which was progressively used as strange or extraordinary instead of a characteristic of a phenomenon.[33]

This changing language use was part of the wider transformation of British society, mentioned in the Introduction, which created a nation led by entrepreneurs, philanthropists, politicians and other thinkers, who, before doubts arose during the 1870s, had grown confident about their progress, the country's prosperity and its leading position in the world. This establishment remade the country, creating many new institutions based on novel concepts of civil service and pride, but also with innovative ideas about the possibilities of learning and science. The elite encouraged codification of the language, which was anchored in the publication of new dictionaries. For example, Richardson's *New English Dictionary (*1835–1837) followed Johnson's work. And in 1858 the Philological Society issued a resolution calling for a new dictionary with every word found in English. The first instalment, covering the letter A, appeared in 1884. By 1900 new volumes extended the cover to H. The final section was published in 1928. Originally known as *A New English Dictionary on Historical Principles*, in 1895 *The Oxford English Dictionary* was added to the title.

The higher middle classes largely embraced the standard variety of British English. Lower middle classes were perhaps even more anxious about language use – their insecurity about social status could be reflected in a nervousness about using what was perceived as improper English, which they wanted to avoid because its use could stigmatise them. During the first decennia of the twentieth century rising social groups, such as civil servants and other white-collar workers, would follow their example and clasp the standard variety.

In general, the new social stratification caused a shift in the character of the word stock of British English from Germanic words to those of Latin and French origin. The reason was a preference in the establishment and aspiring groups for words that had come from Latin and French, because these types of words tended to belong to the domains associated with power and prestige. For example, the Germanic verb to ask was informal, common and warm, while the verb to request came from Latin and French, and was formal, unusual and neutral. However, in everyday speech Germanic or simplified words remained popular, and for instance, as noted by *The Times*, bicycle became bike, because it had a 'Teutonic' sound.[34]

It is feasible that, as a result of this shift in the character of the word stock, alien became more widely used. It was a more formal word of Latin and French origin, suitable for establishment use, and in everyday parlance it was perhaps simpler to say than its synonyms and alternatives, also stemming from Latin and French, such as foreigner, stranger, immigrant and non-native. However, that begs the question why the place of the word alien in public use was not taken by words of Germanic origin. Perhaps most words older than alien, which came from Old English and were of Germanic or Scandinavian origin, were no longer in use or had lost their meaning as foreigner and stranger. Or perhaps, like guest, they had gained a positive meaning and were unsuitable as alternatives for alien if the meaning of that word was being degraded.

Standardisation also felt the effect of other processes of change highlighted in the Introduction. Industrialisation, urbanisation and innovation in the means of communication also had an impact on language use, as people worked and lived closer together and more of them spoke and wrote to more others. Implementation of the standard variety of British English took place in schools. Compulsory elementary education exposed children more than before to the standard, which was prescribed almost universally in British schools, although the manner of instruction was often determined by local teachers and their preferences, which were regularly presented to pupils through grammars and textbooks that stipulated what was perceived as correct or proper language use. Other products of the printing press, such as novels, left their mark. Implementation of the standard variety was also shaped by mass media, foremost the newspapers. Journalists popularised words and meanings, contributing to standardisation. This was further prompted by the time pressure the reporters suffered. In their constant race to beat the deadline, journalists occasionally coined a new word or phrase, but more often than not they repeated readily available terms and clichés, rather than searching for new words or ways of using words. Some journalists also felt the need to be interesting and racy, and they adopted an informal and colloquial style, which trickled down into standard British English. War also enriched the English vocabulary, with a new word being *khaki* (borrowed from Hindi), the colour of the battle dress of the British army during the Second South African War.[35]

Finally, standardisation of British English was an indicator of as well as a contributor to national identity. As standard speech spread more quickly, specific words and meanings were disseminated across the British population. Despite being relatively small, the presence of immigrants influenced the development of British English. They brought words with them, which occasionally found a place in English usage, such as lager and kosher. However, as will be discussed later, the perceived results of their presence also influenced language use.

In short, for people living in Britain between 1841 and 1921 an alien meant most likely a foreigner, stranger or somebody born abroad, possibly an Irish native, and specifically a person residing or working in Britain who did not have British nationality or citizenship. 'Alien' was a borrowed word, experienced in a wide range of contexts during the period under review. This period coincided with the standardisation of British English, which was affected by industrialisation, urbanisation, growing literacy and newspaper reading, and new journalism. It is possible that consequently a more generalised perception of the original meaning of alien arose, certainly broader than a legal concept. Alien maintained a variety of senses, but these meanings could be extended, for instance, from somebody who did not have British nationality or citizenship to a foreigner, stranger or immigrant, and how such a person was perceived and how people felt about that person. Alien was most likely a subject of pejoration and its sense was degraded. It was definitely not an old word getting a new meaning, but while the use of some of its meanings (perhaps temporarily) declined, the affective meaning with negative associations may have been used more often. The frequency of this use is analysed in the next chapter.

Chapter 2

QUANTITATIVE ANALYSIS OF THE USE OF ALIEN

This quantitative analysis examines the changes that occurred in the use of 'alien' and the alternatives for this word between 1841 and 1921. For this purpose it reviews five selected newspapers. This review is placed within a context of other publications. At present, there is no single comprehensive searchable corpus of all British English publications for the period under review. For this reason, a choice has been made for a mixture of collections containing census reports, British English books, parliamentary records and pamphlets, and newspapers. This mixture does not give the entire context, but at least it offers a flavour.

Census reports

The census rarely used the word alien before 1921.[1] Since 1841 it recorded birthplaces with a special box for foreign-born people, for example, marked 'Foreign Parts' in 1841 and 'Foreign Countries' in 1901.[2] The census report of 1851 deviated from this pattern when it commented on the Great Exhibition in London's Crystal Palace attracting many foreigners but listed their number in a table called 'Aliens and Foreigners Reported by Captains of Ships'.[3] The 1861 report avoided the word alien and mentioned the number of 'Subjects of Foreign States' and spoke about 'foreigners by birth'.[4] In his 1871 report the Registrar General wrote that Britain contained 'representatives of nearly all the civilized nations, who have voluntarily sought these shores for the sake of trade, or have been driven at various times by persecution to a land which has ever been […] the sacred asylum and the inviolable home of freedom'.[5]

The word alien reappeared in the report on the census of 1901, when it discussed figures of persons born in foreign countries, for example, their geographical distribution across Britain and their occupations.[6] This report, published in 1903, was written by Registrar General William Dunbar, and he related and possibly responded to the meetings or the report of the Royal Commission on Alien Immigration. The census report applied a mixture of terms and phrases, such as 'aliens', 'alien immigrants', 'foreign-born', 'foreign [...] resident', 'inhabitants [...] born in foreign countries' and 'foreigners'.[7] In 1911 the census report returned to omitting the term alien and applying the previously used category of 'Foreigners'.[8]

The 1921 census used the word alien but did not apply it consistently. The 1921 report provided, for example, tables on 'Foreign-born Population of Alien and Unstated Nationality by Occupation', 'Aliens by Country of Birth and Nationality' and 'Birthplaces of Persons of Foreign Nationality, 1901, 1911 and 1921'.[9] In a few instances the report used alien meaning not having the British nationality. For example, in a passage on British women who had married foreign nationals, 'These, in 1911, were treated as "British by parentage", whereas in 1921, in the absence of a separate category for the class, they have been regarded as more alien to those who, originally alien, have acquired British nationality.' A little further on the report stated, 'in view of the excitement of public feeling regarding the status of aliens during and immediately after the war'. And: 'It is a little doubtful whether our statistical knowledge of aliens in the country has been greatly extended'. Or: 'The rule, treating foreign-born persons of unstated nationality as equivalent to aliens'.[10] The 1921 report probably used alien as a synonym for foreigner when the author wanted to be precise and sought to distinguish between British citizens or subjects and people born abroad who were not British citizens or subjects.

The census reporters were aware of the demographical pressures, but – apart from 1861 – the frequency in their use of the word alien seems not to have been related with the number of foreigners recorded in Britain. In the 1901 census report the authors may have responded to a contemporary debate. It is possible that between 1841 and 1911 they wanted to avoid the term alien and only reluctantly used it. Throughout the entire period before 1921 they appear to have had problems with classifying foreign-born persons in Britain, and perhaps this resulted from the lack of a clear and consistent legal definition of British citizenship, as discussed previously. However, it is also feasible that the registrars simply emulated the changing use of the word alien, which can be verified by the following quantitative analysis of that use in other British English publications and parliamentary records.

British English literature

Google Books is one of the largest searchable language corpora. Other examples are the British National Corpus, the British Academic Written English and the Scottish Corpus of Texts and Speech. Google Books is used here because it contains British English publications from various dates and

Table 2. The number of uses in the Google Books corpus of British English publications

	Aliens	**Refugees**	**Immigrants**	**Strangers**	**Foreigners**
1840–49	3,781	3,030	833	46,019	24,260
1850–59	3,242	5,154	2,086	47,752	25,852
1860–69	3,747	3,830	2,706	41,543	23,567
1870–79	4,339	5,777	4,643	49,753	26,805
1880–89	4,706	6,570	6,611	52,626	31,171
1890–99	6,353	7,416	8,374	52,531	35,540
1900–1909	9,202	8,865	9,544	55,242	48,134
1910–19	4,130	5,996	5,956	19,301	17,839

across the globe, in early 2019 containing some 34 billion words printed in works of fiction and non-fiction.[11] It enables measurement of the use of a word in a specific period. The results of a search for the word aliens and alternatives for this word are listed in Table 2.

Table 2 denotes that in 1840–49 'aliens' appeared 3,781 times. This figure dropped in the next decennium, but it rose again steadily after that, to jump up in 1890–99 and 1900–1909, coinciding with an accelerated growth in immigration and debates on the legislation to restrict alien immigration, after which it fell. This last drop coincides with the slower growth and decline in the number of foreigners in Britain, but the decrease has to remain unexplained, because it could also have been caused by a general decline in publishing during the First World War years due to paper shortage, distribution problems and other issues.

Table 2 also includes figures on alternatives for the word aliens. They are refugees, strangers, immigrants and foreigners. Two alternatives that are not examined in this quantitative analysis are outsiders and non-natives. The main reason for omitting outsiders is that the word grew enormously popular in the period between 1841 and 1921,[12] but had come to mean something totally different. Outsider was very often not used in the sense of a person from outside a specific community, but as a competitor who was not expected to win, for example, in well-liked sports such as horse racing, which completely distorts the figures and prevents proper interpretation. In contrast, non-native was used so little as a noun that it can be overlooked here. For example, *The Times* did not apply it as a noun from 1841 until 1863, when the paper reported a court case concerning a dispute about Oxford and Cambridge scholarships for boys who attended Wakefield Grammar School: 'Mr Fitzherbert Ashley, who was a non-native, so to speak',[13] which meant he was not a native of Wakefield. Later, between 1890 and 1919, *The Times* used

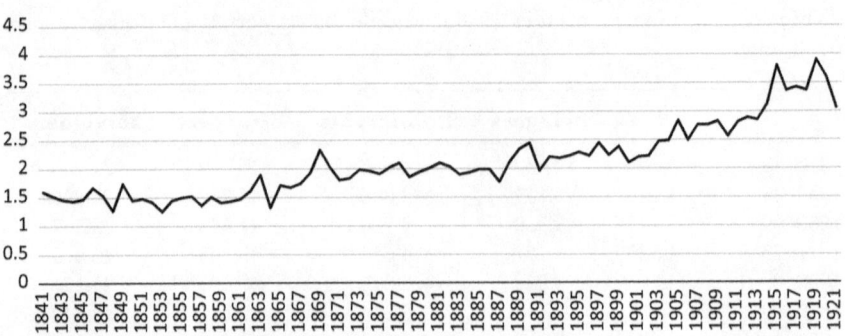

Figure 1. The frequency of the word alien in a corpus of British English literature, 1841–1921

non-native on 14 occasions as a noun. In comparison, the *Daily Mail* did not apply it as a noun before 1919.

Omitting outsiders and non-natives, Table 2 points towards a decrease in the use of the other alternatives in the decennium 1910–19, which mirrored the declining use of alien, but reviewed over the entire period between 1840 and 1909, the use of all words rose significantly; that of immigrants increased more than tenfold. Noteworthy in this sample is that with a few exceptions, the alternatives almost consistently outnumbered aliens.

However, the figures in Table 2 fail to provide information on the relative importance of these developments, because they measure appearance in a body of work that is changing in size. In addition, the contents of Google Books cannot be adjusted to make more representative samples, for example, consisting entirely of novels published in Britain. These shortcomings can be partly rectified by analysing the Collins online dictionary,[14] which provides data on trends in the use of the words. The Collins word data are based on information from Google n-grams,[15] available from 1708 to 2008. The data represent the relative frequency of words and give the value of that frequency in a specific year. This information comes from a corpus of British English works, some published in Britain and some in the United States. However, the data is biased in terms of selection of specific genres, such as scientific literature, and therefore only paints a rough picture. It is presented graphically in Figure 1.

Figure 1 shows the frequency of all words in this corpus that include the string 'alien'. It clearly indicates an upward trend in the use of alien between 1841 and 1921. Overall, the frequency was low – always lower than four – but it went up, more than doubling in the period under review. In more detail, in 1841 the frequency was 1.60, down from previous high points in 1714 (3.04)

Table 3. The number of uses in Britain's parliament according to Hansard

	Alien or Aliens	Refugee or Refugees	Immigrant or Immigrants	Stranger or Strangers	Foreigner or Foreigners
1840–49	194	108	90	246	1,571
1850–59	295	366	74	270	1,402
1860–69	201	98	40	206	980
1870–79	262	143	70	308	768
1880–89	777	197	87	508	989
1890–99	888	127	296	355	1,152
1900–1909	2,688	346	1,166	260	2,577
1910–19	6,197	380	202	202	1,376

and 1791 (3.43). After 1841 it dropped slightly, to rise again in 1845 (1.47), 1846 (1.67) and 1849 (1.74), following perhaps the increased arrival of political refugees from continental Europe. Then the frequency decreased again somewhat, hovered for a while around the 1841 figure, and rose to 1.89 in 1863. After 1865 it remained well above the 1841 figure, overall increasing to 2.44 in 1897. The rise continued for most of the years after 1903 to reach 3.90 in 1919, coinciding with the public debates about the restriction of alien immigration and the First World War alien legislation. For the rest of the twentieth century the frequency would remain poised around three.

Taken together, the Google and Collins details point towards a slow but steady increase in the use of alien in British English literature from the middle of the nineteenth century, with higher growth towards the end of the century.

Parliamentary record and pamphlets

The Google Books corpus includes some of Hansard, the edited verbatim report of proceedings of the House of Commons and the House of Lords. The entire Hansard is available in digital format on ProQuest's House of Commons Parliamentary Papers,[16] which contain a vast archive of official government documents and related papers that dates back to the eighteenth century. The spoken parliamentary record, recorded in Hansard, which reflected as well as formed public opinion, can be analysed separately.[17] A semantic search for instances in which 'alien' or 'aliens' and instances when alternatives were mentioned in parliament provides detailed figures, which are listed in Table 3.

Table 3 shows that in 1840–49 the words alien and aliens were uttered 194 times in parliament. The use of these words rose during the next decennium,

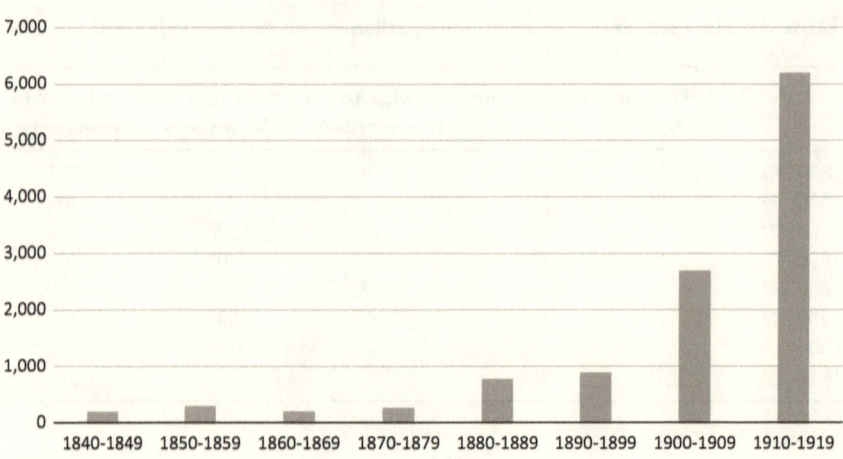

Figure 2. The use of the words alien and aliens in Britain's parliament

but it fell after that. However, then the number of instances more than trebled and rose significantly in 1900–1909 and explosively in 1910–19, the decennia that brought the political debate on aliens and new legislation before, during and after the First World War.

These words and some of their alternatives had been used in parliament before 1841. For example, the first nineteenth-century use of the word aliens in parliament was made in 1806 in relation to legislation on foreigners. Three years earlier alien was used meaning different, distinct or directly opposed to. In 1805 came an Alien Bill and a year later a parliamentarian said you could not exempt somebody from taxation, just because that person was an alien. The word refugees was first used during the nineteenth century in 1805, in relation to refugees in Ireland, after that it referred to other groups such as French, German and protestant refugees. Refugee first appeared in 1814, related to a French person. However, the first use of the word immigrants dated to early 1842, when privation and distress in the colonies were described and mention was made of labour competition from immigrants in these colonies. Immigrant was first used in 1843 on similar issues.

The Hansard trend for 1841–1921 relating to the use of the words alien and aliens is illustrated graphically in Figure 2.

Figure 2 not only confirms, but also accentuates the earlier findings on the rise of the word alien. It reveals a first significant rise in 1880–89 compared to the previous decennium. In this period alien was used in the Commons when parliament discussed immigrants in the United Kingdom, for example,

Table 4. The number of uses of specific words in British Library Nineteenth-Century British Pamphlets

	An Alien or Aliens	A Refugee or Refugees	An Immigrant or Immigrants	A Stranger or Strangers	A Foreigner or Foreigners
1840–49	487	26	64	1,070	445
1850–59	744	73	66	1,532	519
1860–69	1,088	79	105	1,445	620
1870–79	1,395	68	136	1,714	724
1880–89	2,031	108	232	2,027	901
1890–99	3,663	162	561	2,287	1,249
1900–1909	6,034	290	1,153	3,028	1,501
1910–19	6,125	353	1,758	3,220	1,765

in 1880 in relation to Rumanian Jews, in 1882 in relation to US citizens in Ireland, and in 1887 in relation to the naturalisation of aliens.

Table 3 also offers figures on the number of times when alternatives for alien and aliens were used in parliament. They indicate that, while the use of alien and aliens largely increased, at first steadily and then explosively, the use of the alternatives varied. Noteworthy is the rising use of immigrant and immigrants in 1890–1909 before it dropped in 1910–19. In contrast to Table 2, Table 3 reveals that after 1900 the use of alien or aliens in Britain's parliament outnumbered the use of all alternatives.

Throughout the nineteenth century pamphlets were important means of public debate on the political issues of the day as well as prominent subjects in other fields, such as science. The British Library collection Nineteenth-Century British Pamphlets contains about 26,000 pamphlets digitised from collections of seven universities across the United Kingdom, containing more than a million pages. This collection may not be representative of all British pamphlets in the nineteenth century – too much depends on the nature of the contributions and selection criteria – but it provides a notion of the use of words in public debate about political issues. The results of a search in this collection using the strings 'an alien' or 'aliens', 'a foreigner' or 'foreigners', and 'an immigrant' or 'immigrants' are presented in Table 4.

These figures are slightly misleading when it comes to aliens in Britain. This is due to the methodology of the available search programme. The search results include the word 'alienigenae'[18] and an article in the journal *Scientific American*, which was titled 'A Foreigner's Impression of America' but does not appear to contain the word alien. Nevertheless, Table 4 suggests that the presence of aliens and their immigration were often topics of political debate.[19]

This was not a new phenomenon. Earlier pamphlets can be found in a digital format in the Gale Seventeenth- and Eighteenth-Century Nichols Newspapers Collection, with about 300 news titles and a similar number of pamphlets. A search in that corpus reveals that in the centuries that preceded the period under review, 13 monographs and 3,110 entries in newspapers and periodicals used the word aliens or its alternatives, mostly foreigners. They included a one-page address from 1679 titled 'To the Kings Most Excellent Majesty': 'there hath been, and is, a Hellish, Popish Conspiracy, to destroy Your Majesty, the Protestant Religion, and Government; and to that end a Correspondence between Persons in this Kingdom, and Foreigners, for which several are Impeached' and a treatise from 1720 called 'The Case of the Italian Merchants Importing Goods of the Growth of Asia, by way of Italy'. Obviously, political debate about foreigners in Britain was not new in 1840.

The members of parliament who in the period 1841–1921 most used the word aliens in their speeches were – ranked by the number of uses – William Joynson-Hicks; John Butcher, Edward Shortt, Reginald McKenna and Aretas Akers-Douglas. The Conservative Joynson-Hicks used aliens 257 times from 1913. He served in parliament intermittently from 1908 and filled government posts after 1921. Butcher was also a Conservative. He used aliens 210 times from 1913. The Liberal Shortt became a cabinet member in 1918 and was, more significantly for his 143 times use of aliens, home secretary from 1919 to 1922. The next in the number of uses was the Liberal McKenna, who served as financial secretary to the treasury, president of the Board of Education, first lord of the Admiralty, home secretary and chancellor of the Exchequer. He used aliens 143 times from 1904, when during that year he asked questions about pauper aliens in Britain. He used the word again in 1911, when he spoke about criminal aliens. Finally, the Conservative Akers-Douglas used aliens 142 times from 1896, usually in relation to immigrants in the United Kingdom.

As will be discussed later, a few members of parliament dominated press reports on the political debates about aliens in Britain. Among them was the Conservative Howard (or Charles) Vincent. In this ranking he comes sixteenth, using aliens 85 times from 1890, when he referred to *The Times* writing about 'The Invasion of Pauper Aliens'.[20] In 1903 he introduced a bill for the exclusion and deportation of criminal aliens.[21] Another, and lower-ranking parliamentarian in terms of the numerical use of aliens, was the Conservative William Evans-Gordon, MP for Stepney, who uttered the word aliens 64 times from 1902, when he spoke about destitute aliens.

However, all these politicians also spoke about other subjects than aliens and some spoke more than others. When ranked by the relevance of the use of the word aliens in their entire spoken contribution to parliament, the Conservative Horatio Davies came first. However, he used aliens only once in 1905, when he asked whether there were aliens in the Durham mines, which simply means he did not often address parliament from his seat in the House. The second highest ranking in relevance was the Liberal Stuart Samuel, MP for Whitechapel and elder brother of the later Home Secretary Herbert Samuel.[22] He used aliens 45 times from 1902, when he said that as the representative of a constituency in which a large number of those aliens resided, he welcomed a government inquiry on the subject. In 1905 he opposed Conservatives who argued that in the East End of London 'hordes' of aliens were driving the British workman away. Samuel also maintained that the Jewish immigrants were not a burden on public funds, as they were supported by the Jewish community. He pointed out that the allegations made against aliens were not based on facts: 'No figures of any authority had been produced; but, nevertheless, again and again, the [supporters or restriction of immigration] had referred to the pauperism of aliens in this country.'[23] Earlier, Samuel had published an article for the *Economic Journal*, which reviewed the wider context, implications and future of immigration. Ranking in terms of relevance William Evans-Gordon was 11th and Howard Vincent came 71st.

It can be concluded that the MPs who used the word aliens most often, frequently spoke about this subject in the twentieth century. They came from both sides of the House. Of the high scorers, only Akers-Douglas and Vincent used it earlier in parliament, that is, during the 1890s. With a few exceptions the use of aliens was often related to the constituency or post in government of these MPs, for example, because many aliens were present in the constituency or the post meant a large involvement with issues concerning aliens.

Newspapers

The context presented so far indicates that the use of alien by authors of books and politicians in Britain grew between 1841 and 1921. As newspapers reviewed books and reported on current affairs, such as politics, it can be expected that they mirrored the use of alien by book authors and politicians. The results of searches on newspaper use of alien and alternative words are detailed in Tables 5, 6 and 7.

The British Newspaper Archives is a project to digitise up to 40 million newspaper pages from the British Library's vast collection of historical newspapers, which contains papers from 1603 to the present day, published in Britain and further afield. It was launched in 2011. At the time of the research

Table 5. The number of uses of specific words in the British Newspaper Archive

	An Alien or Aliens	A Refugee or Refugees	An Immigrant or Immigrants	A Stranger or Strangers	A Foreigner or Foreigners
1840–49	100,444	702	17,040	35,717	52,721
1850–59	123,044	2,039	30,814	54,916	93,740
1860–69	201,340	2,115	40,399	77,241	121,672
1870–79	180,992	1,465	39,229	59,633	89,160
1880–89	261,345	1,965	57,749	84,043	100,698
1890–99	323,521	1,695	61,557	78,470	93,357
1900–1909	419,785	2,297	82,608	68,415	85,500
1910–19	282,911	2,019	32,843	31,968	44,654

that was conducted for this book[24] the British Newspaper Archive project had scanned millions of pages of newspapers, with hundreds of millions of articles. At that time, the Archive contained about 1,200 titles with many papers from cities such as Birmingham, Manchester, Glasgow, Nottingham, Derby and Leicester, along with local papers from London, including the *Glasgow Herald* (from 1820 to 1900), the *London Evening Standard* (from 1827 to 1909) and the *Nottingham Evening Post* (from 1878), but not *The Times* and the *Daily Mail* (they can be found separately in the Gale collections). This corpus contains relatively many regional and local newspapers, but still provides one of the largest accessible samples of the UK press in the period under review.

The numbers in Table 5 include results that can also be found separately in the pre-existing Nineteenth-Century British Library Newspapers collection, a digitised collection of 48 national and regional newspapers from England, Wales, Scotland and Ireland, which is possibly less biased towards the local press. This collection was searched too and the results are listed in Table 6.[25]

Combined, Tables 5 and 6 show that between 1840 and 1919 the use of the words an alien or aliens in newspapers more than doubled, while it rose relatively higher in British newspapers in the British Library collection. These increases were uneven, with dips between 1850 and 1859 in the British Library collection and between 1870 and 1879 in the British Newspaper Archive, which in 1870–79 could have been related to a slower rise in immigration during a period of economic depression but remain largely unexplained. The growing use of a refugee, refugees, an immigrant and immigrants, while rising overall between 1840 and 1919, is similarly uneven. Noticeable in the uneven figures on foreigner and foreigners is the drop after 1899, accentuated after 1909. On the use of a stranger and strangers, it can be concluded that

Table 6. The number of uses of specific words in Nineteenth-Century British Library Newspapers

	An Alien or Aliens	A Refugee or Refugees	An Immigrant or Immigrants	A Stranger or Strangers	A Foreigner or Foreigners
1840–49	28	75	7	39	58
1850–59	9	416	10	245	154
1860–69	7	46	8	280	232
1870–79	14	205	50	140	176
1880–89	55	287	93	213	431
1890–99	293	452	124	206	507
1900–1909	837	286	180	110	367
1910–19	948	888	70	47	129

overall these words were used less in 1919 than in 1840 in the papers of British Newspaper Archive and less in 1919 than in 1860 in the papers of the British Library collection.

The use of these words was in 1840 not new in the papers of the British Newspaper Archive or a novelty of the nineteenth century. 'An alien' or 'aliens' had already been used 18,560 times between 1750 and 1799. Similarly, the following terms occurred between 1750 and 1799: a refugee or refugees 47 times; an immigrant or immigrants 51 times; a stranger or strangers 736 times; and a foreigner or foreigners 6,800 times.

So far, few if any far-reaching conclusions can be drawn from Tables 5 and 6, simply because they cover so many and a changing total of newspapers with varying numbers of pages and articles contained in these papers. More can be achieved by advanced searches in the digital collections of the five selected British papers with more stable page and article numbers. The results of these searches are listed in Table 7.

The search of the digital archive of *The Times*,[26] the results of which are shown in Table 7, brings out that in the decennium 1840–49 this paper used 'an alien' or 'aliens' 367 times. After a dip in 1850–59, the use rose to 3,128 in 1910–19, with the most noticeable instances of growth after 1880. The paper's use of a refugee or refugees also rose overall between 1840 and 1919, but from 1900 onwards it was used less than an alien or aliens. The use of an immigrant or immigrants in *The Times* rose but remained under the level of an alien, aliens, a refugee and refugees, and it dropped significantly after 1909. Remarkable is also that the use of a stranger, strangers, a foreigner and foreigners, which had vastly surpassed the combined number of the other three alternatives in 1840, fell to below the level of an alien or aliens between 1910 and 1919.

It is impossible to compare the use in *The Times* with the other selected newspapers for the entire period. The *London Evening Standard*,[27] the *Glasgow Herald*,[28] the *Nottingham Evening Post*[29] and the *Daily Mail*[30] were not published during the entire period under review or their digitised records are unavailable for some the years between 1840 and 1919. Nevertheless, the figures in Table 7 signify that the use of 'an alien' or 'aliens' in all papers in the course of the available years overtook the use of the alternatives. The fall in use of all these words in the *Nottingham Evening Post* in 1910–19, with the exception of a refugee or refugees, may have been partly caused by that newspaper losing pages as a possible result of wartime paper shortages, printing problems and other publication issues or errors in digitisation. It also appears that the *London Evening Standard* used an alien or aliens as well as an immigrant or immigrants more than *The Times*, but it applied the other alternatives less than *The Times*. This may have resulted from different coverage of issues related to these words, such as foreign news, notably on military conflicts abroad, or simply from more pages or editions of the *Standard* papers being included in the digital archive.[31]

Tables 5, 6 and 7 provide information on the use of alien as a noun in British newspapers, but they include articles that mentioned the word but may not have had aliens as their main subject. An advanced search for a combination of the strings 'an alien' and 'aliens' – where an article contained both strings – narrows down the results to pieces that were more likely to have aliens as their subject. This search also includes alternatives for an alien and aliens, such as a foreigner and foreigners. It is conducted for *The Times* and the *Daily Mail*.[32] The results are reproduced in Table 8.

Table 8 shows the number of occasions on which a combination of the strings 'an alien' and 'aliens' occurred, and as a result, these are relatively low figures. They reveal several outstanding trends in how often the two newspapers wrote about aliens. In 1840–49 *The Times* used the string combination 24 times. This increased in the next decennium, but fell, then stabilised and rose in 1880–89, but again dropped in 1890–99, rose again and then more than doubled in 1910–19. The paper's combined use of a foreigner and foreigners was greater in 1840–49 than an alien and aliens, increased until 1879, but then fell, so that by 1919 it was much lower than the use of an alien and aliens. The use of a stranger and strangers followed a similar pattern. An immigrant and immigrants shot up in 1900–1909, while a refugee and refugees occurred in varying degrees, but in significant numbers throughout the period between 1840 and 1919. These changes are echoed in the *Daily Mail* figures, available for 1900–1919, although that paper used an alien and aliens relatively more often. The trends in *The Times* are visualised in Figure 3.

Table 7. Number of uses in selected British newspapers

	1840–49	1850–59	1860–69	1870–79	1880–89	1890–99	1900–1909	1910–19
The Times								
an alien or aliens	367	349	456	482	844	1,327	1,970	3,128
a refugee or refugees	779	1,170	654	1,224	1,032	1,443	1,712	2,540
an immigrant or immigrants	202	405	487	575	726	696	1,257	806
a stranger or strangers	3,462	3,392	3,863	3,654	3,551	2,320	1,991	1,561
a foreigner or foreigners	2,883	3,939	4,385	4,162	4,654	4,638	5,349	2,796
London Evening Standard								
an alien or aliens	1,272	1,371	5,692	2,716	2,854	3,217	6,900	
a refugee or refugees	17	53	72	39	31	57	40	
an immigrant or immigrants	361	495	1,415	1,028	1,326	1,288	3,070	
a stranger or strangers	844	905	1,635	1,020	840	807	361	
a foreigner or foreigners	1,749	2,425	4,598	2,665	2,275	2,185	1,427	
Glasgow Herald								
an alien or aliens	397	469	1,106	1,498	2,751	3,309		
a refugee or refugees	6	24	24	14	20	46		
an immigrant or immigrants	116	243	405	442	583	903		
a stranger or strangers	173	358	718	579	759	708		
a foreigner or foreigners								
Nottingham Evening Post								
an alien or aliens					782	1,015	2,606	1,886
a refugee or refugees					16	7	16	22
an immigrant or immigrants					293	431	769	342
a stranger or strangers					393	269	359	209
a foreigner or foreigners					448	379	552	386

(continued)

Table 7. (*cont.*)

	1840–49	1850–59	1860–69	1870–79	1880–89	1890–99	1900–1909	1910–19
Daily Mail								
an alien or aliens							1,082	1,930
a refugee or refugees							679	1,001
an immigrant or immigrants							387	200
a stranger or strangers							1,837	1,233
a foreigner or foreigners							2,578	1,259

Table 8. Number of uses in *The Times* and *Daily Mail*

	1840–49	1850–59	1860–69	1870–79	1880–89	1890–99	1900–1909	1910–19
The Times								
an alien and aliens	24	33	26	26	62	46	105	290
a foreigner and foreigners	75	132	151	170	136	136	122	56
a stranger and strangers	106	101	120	129	125	62	46	37
an immigrant and immigrants	1	3	3	6	9	7	46	21
a refugee and refugees	20	47	17	15	14	24	37	45
Total	226	316	317	346	346	275	356	449
Daily Mail								
an alien and aliens							34	128
a foreigner and foreigners							50	23
a stranger and strangers							59	33
an immigrant and immigrants							12	6
a refugee and refugees							4	19
Total							159	209

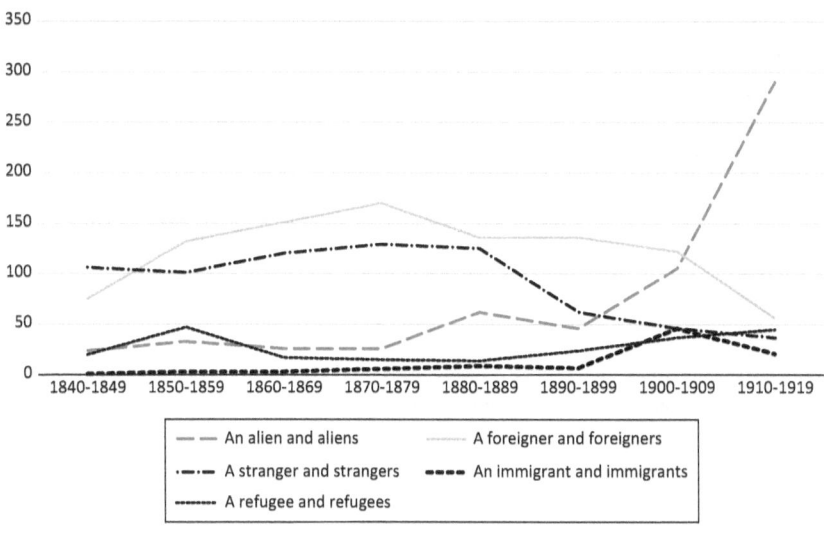

Figure 3. Trends in word choice in *The Times*, 1840–1919

Figure 3 signifies that, viewed over the whole period, the paper's use of the noun alien(s) overtook the use of the nouns foreigner(s) and stranger(s). This rise became explosive after 1900, when the paper's use of the noun immigrant(s) also rose, first in a similar way but then less spectacular. Two different, although smaller, but still noticeable changes are the rising use of alien(s) in 1850–59, coinciding with the rise of refugee(s) and foreigner(s), and the increase of alien(s) in 1880–89, coinciding with the decline of foreigner(s). Overall, this emphasises that when the paper increasingly applied alien(s) it used the words foreigner(s) and stranger(s) less – notably in specific periods of time, namely 1880–89 and 1900–1919, at times of accelerating immigration, debate about restriction of alien immigration and the position of aliens during and after the First World War.

To sum up, the conclusions that can be drawn from the quantitative analysis are limited by the lack of consistently robust and comparable data. Nevertheless, it is clear that overall the use of the word alien in British literature, parliamentary record and newspaper publication rose significantly between 1840 and 1919. At times this growth was more substantial than at other times, notably at the end of the nineteenth and beginning of the twentieth century. In newspapers, this rise appeared at the cost of alternatives such as foreigner, which was used relatively less by 1919. This shift in the newspapers' use of these words also occurred in politics, notable through parliamentary debate and pamphlets, but it was not emulated in British English literature. Perhaps this happened as newspapers more than books reported and commentated on the outstanding political issues of the day, such as immigration. As the growth in the number of foreign-born people in Britain accelerated, the noun immigrant was also used much more often in the early twentieth century than in 1841. Perhaps the rising use of alien was related to the growing number of people living in Britain who had not been born here, including those who were regarded as immigrants. However, immigrants had been in Britain for a long time, and it seems as if at the start of the period under review they were not often mentioned in publications, or if they were discussed, they were named foreigners. Obviously, by 1921 something had changed and other factors than the growing immigrant presence increasingly caused them to be called aliens rather than foreigners. These factors are analysed in the next chapter.

Chapter 3

QUALITATIVE ANALYSIS OF THE USE OF ALIEN

In 1921, more people in Britain more often read the word alien than in 1841. This qualitative analysis determines how the use of alien in newspapers developed during this period, what it meant and which overtones it acquired.

The tables presented so far do not list separately the use of the word alien as a noun and as an adjective. As stated, the adjective alien can mean foreign, strange or different, distinct and opposed to, and may not be related to foreigners, strangers and aliens. To investigate this further, an advanced search in *The Times* for the string 'alien' has been made, with a manual check of all the articles found through this search, to determine the specific uses and meanings of alien. The results of that examination are listed in Table 9.

Table 9 shows that the paper only very sparingly applied alien as a verb, meaning to quarrel; a legal term for a specific action, meaning the transfer of property; a botanical term,[1] meaning of foreign origin or growth; and a linguistic term, meaning borrowed from another language. The use of all these meanings together always constituted less than half a per cent of the total use in a specific period. The table also indicates that the use of alien as an adjective and noun meaning foreign(er) and strange(r) between 1841 and 1890 surpassed and after 1890 greatly exceeded the use of alien as an adjective meaning different, distinct and opposed to, which actually declined after 1890. The figures in Table 9 also enable the conclusion that the spectacular rise of alien in *The Times* after 1890 can be contributed to the application of this word to foreigners and strangers who were in Britain. And when the data in Tables 8 and 9 are combined, it is obvious that the rising uses of alien and immigrant coincided.

The data from Table 9 are graphically reproduced in Figure 4.

Figure 4 brings out the major trends in the use and meaning of alien in *The Times* between 1841 and 1920. Five periods can be distinguished:

- 1841–60 with little overall change;
- 1861–80 with a rise in the meaning of foreign(er) and strange(r) as well as that of distinct, different and opposed to;

Table 9. The use and meaning of the word alien in *The Times*, 1841–1920

	Found	Meaning Foreign(er), Strange(r) in General	Of which Meaning Foreigner, Stranger in Britain	Meaning Distinct, Different, Opposed to	Other Meanings
1841–50	370	217	43	149	4
1851–60	352	210	35	141	1
1861–70	618	331	17	282	5
1871–80	679	352	14	324	3
1881–90	1,049	571	96	471	7
1891–1900	1,323	911	361	405	7
1901–10	1,841	1,443	867	389	9
1911–20	2,805	2,470	1,567	328	7

- 1881–90 with further rises in both meanings as well as the meaning of foreigner and stranger in Britain;
- 1891–1910 with sharper rises in the meanings of foreign(er) and strange(r) and foreigner and stranger in Britain, accompanied by a slow decline in the meaning of distinct, different and opposed to; and
- 1911–20 with even greater rises in the meanings of foreign(er) and strange(r) and foreigner and stranger in Britain, and a further but smaller decline in the meaning of distinct, different and opposed to.

Although there is no doubt that prejudice already existed well before the start of the period under review,[2] it does not lie within the scope of this book to analyse attitudes among native-born people towards foreigners in Britain before 1841. Instead, what happened to this bias in the five periods outlined above is analysed here. To accommodate this analysis a listing of the results of an advanced search with a manual check of the annual use of two meanings of alien in *The Times* from 1841 to 1921 is provided in Table 10 with a graphic reproduction of the figures in Figure 5.

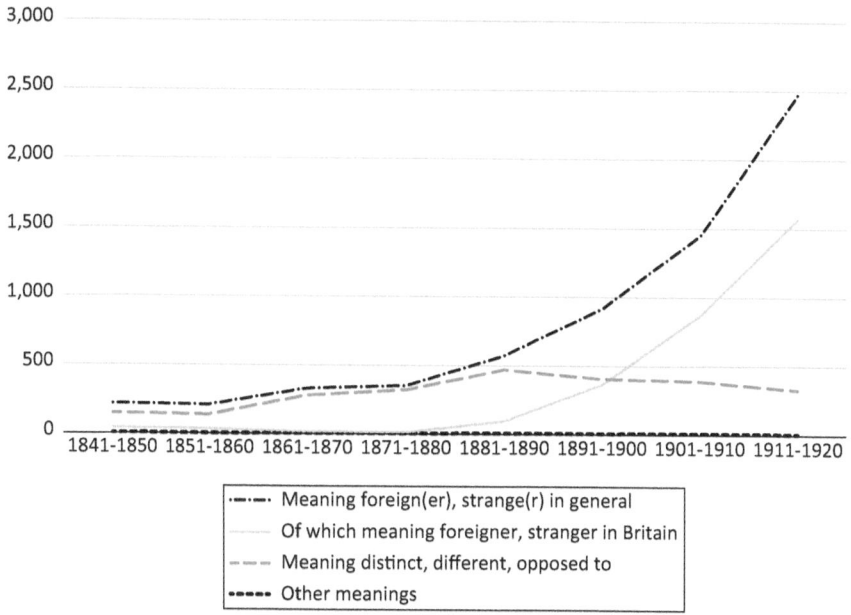

Figure 4. The use and meaning of the word alien in *The Times*, 1841–1920

1841–60

Table 10 shows that in 1841 *The Times* used the word alien no less than 34 times: 18 uses meant foreign(er) or strange(r), including 1 reference to a German and 7 to people with other nationalities who were in Britain;[3] and 16 uses meant different, distinct and opposed to.[4] In the years from 1841 to 1860 the annual use mostly fluctuated around these marks, with notably higher exceptions in 1848 and 1849, a dip in 1852,[5] and a significant rise in 1856, 1857 and 1858.

During this period *The Times* applied the word several times in reports on local judicial courts that dealt with objections raised against the registration of specific voters. For example, in 1841, the paper reported an objection against 'Suseman Abraham' of Petticoat Lane in London 'on the ground of want of occupation and being an alien'.[6] He told the court he was a freeman and liveryman of London and was born there. However, other witnesses testified he was a poor foreigner, born in Holland or Germany. According to a report three days later, in a similar case the court arrived at an argued judgment, making reference to an earlier case and Blackstone's *Commentaries on the Laws of England*. On the basis of Blackstone, the court established that 'aliens are such

Table 10. Meanings of the word alien in *The Times*, 1841–1921

	Total	Foreign(er), Strange(r)	Distinct, Different, Opposed to
1841	34	18	16
1842	25	11	14
1843	30	22	8
1844	38	18	20
1845	33	18	15
1846	31	12	19
1847	30	17	13
1848	64	46	18
1849	47	36	11
1850	34	19	15
1851	27	16	11
1852	17	8	9
1853	29	19	10
1854	27	16	11
1855	29	15	14
1856	40	21	19
1857	56	34	22
1858	68	53	15
1859	27	14	13
1860	31	14	17
1861	41	29	12
1862	40	25	15
1863	47	27	20
1864	36	28	8
1865	46	33	13
1866	47	24	23
1867	64	34	30
1868	122	44	78
1869	89	34	55
1870	81	53	28
1871	57	29	28
1872	52	23	29
1873	55	20	35
1874	59	25	34
1875	74	43	31
1876	62	34	28
1877	75	43	32
1878	68	37	31
1879	78	46	32
1880	96	52	44
1881	83	46	37
1882	110	73	37
1883	109	58	51
1884	87	47	40

Table 10. (*cont.*)

	Total	Foreign(er), Strange(r)	Distinct, Different, Opposed to
1885	92	49	43
1886	129	62	67
1887	114	56	58
1888	114	69	45
1889	92	42	50
1890	112	69	43
1891	131	97	34
1892	136	82	54
1893	127	82	45
1894	160	115	45
1895	129	85	44
1896	109	91	18
1897	152	118	34
1898	138	86	52
1899	140	101	39
1900	94	54	40
1901	122	88	34
1902	177	148	29
1903	216	184	32
1904	243	208	35
1905	217	185	32
1906	193	159	34
1907	162	114	48
1908	163	107	56
1909	146	106	40
1910	193	144	49
1911	268	219	49
1912	157	104	53
1913	167	117	50
1914	319	288	31
1915	356	345	11
1916	278	266	12
1917	250	238	12
1918	417	398	19
1919	357	307	50
1920	229	188	41
1921	187	148	39

as are not born within the dominions of the crown of England', which meant that electors found to be aliens had to be 'expunged' from the list of electors.[7]

In these two reports, the meaning of alien relates to the traditional legal concept, namely a foreigner who does not have the nationality or citizenship of the country in which they live, and hence in Britain they cannot exercise

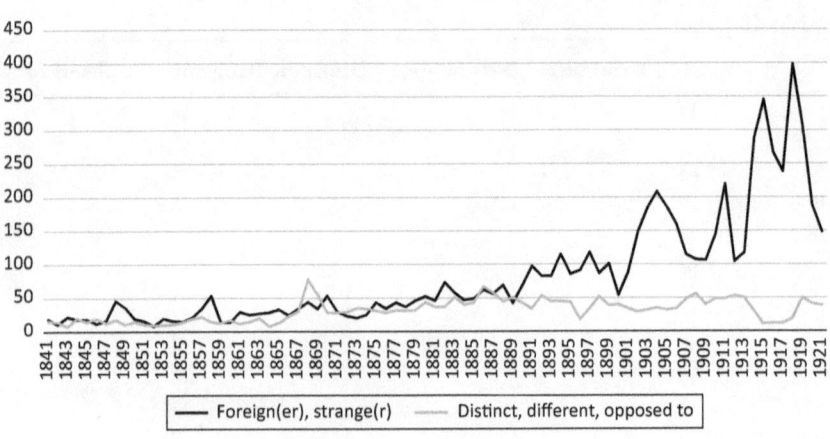

Figure 5. Meanings of the word alien in *The Times*

certain privileges that have been allocated to people who have British nationality or citizenship, such as the right to vote. However, at the time, the alien label was also applied to groups who did have British nationality or citizenship. The journalist who wrote the second report, quoted above, stated that the revising barrister spoke about '*post nati* – that is, those Scots who were born after the union of the crowns of England and Scotland [in 1707] but these parties were not aliens'. This opinion went back to the English 1705 Alien Act, which regarded Scottish-born people in England as aliens. The implication of the barrister's words was that this perception had lingered in English minds. Within Scotland itself some Scots were regarded as aliens. In 1846, the *Glasgow Herald* wrote that the people of the Lowlands had no sympathy with their Highland countrymen, who were 'aliens in blood and language' and regarded as lawless and dangerous.[8]

Irish-born people had come to Britain for centuries but following the famine years between 1845 and 1849 they arrived in greater numbers than before. The Irish could find themselves in a similar position as the Scots in England and the Highlanders in the Scottish Lowlands, which can be illustrated by the earlier used quote from Sir John Davies: 'The mere Irish were not only accounted aliens'.[9] Following Sir John's words, initially the Irish-born residents of Britain may have been perceived as aliens. Furthermore, other people of Irish descent were called aliens. In 1844 the *Glasgow Herald* reported about riots in America, involving 'a horde of Irish, or, as they are termed, alien or naturalised ruffians'.[10] Later, the publicity surrounding the trial of William Burke and William Hare, the Irish murderers who sold the bodies of their victims to the Edinburgh anatomist Robert Knox, accentuated the association of Irish, alien and crime. The *Glasgow Herald* reported that Burke claimed he was a naturalised subject of the United States and 'should be tried by a jury partly composed of foreigners'.[11]

To complicate the analysis of the use of alien, throughout the period 1841–1921, the word was mentioned in public and political debates on Ireland. An editorial in *The Times* said in 1842: 'Ireland feels that she is not an integral portion of the British empire – every act of the British Parliament tells her she is an alien, an outcast, a neglected, an oppressed one.'[12] Later Prime Minister William Gladstone reportedly asked an audience 'whether, supposing they believed Ireland was entitled to a complete national existence, and while prosecuting that end, they found a measure, passed by the so-called alien Parliament, granting liberal privileges and security to the cultivator of the soil, they would, in consequence of their ulterior views, reject the immediate boon'.[13] Gladstone's words 'the so-called alien Parliament' referred to Irish nationalists calling the Westminster parliament 'alien'. Over the years, often at times of elections, in debates on Irish Home Rule and unrest in Ireland, the word was used in this sense by otherwise very different speakers such as Joseph Chamberlain, Randolph Churchill, Charles Parnell and Eamon de Valera.

A similar ambiguity arises in references to an 'alien church',[14] a tag that could be fixed to the Church of England, the Church of Ireland and the Roman Catholic Church, usually by their Christian opponents. Aliens were mentioned in the same breath as Catholics. In 1845, a speaker in the House of Lords said: 'Catholics, not as aliens in blood, in language, [...] entitled to equal rights and privileges, civil and religious'.[15] The tag 'alien church' was used during the debates about the disruption and disestablishment of the churches of Scotland, Wales and Ireland. Aliens were mooted in 1848 during General Assembly of the Free Church of Scotland: 'strangers and aliens had stepped in and taken that which, by the rights and laws of Scotland, belonged to them'.[16] People also spoke about alien priories, meaning the medieval monasteries, where monks had been responsible to papal, not British rulers.

This raises the question what meaning can be attributed to the word alien in these cases. The guideline adopted in this book is that no matter who uses alien in these instances as an adjective, such as in 'an alien parliament', the majority of the readers of *The Times* likely regarded England, Wales, Scotland and Ireland as integral parts of the kingdom, not as foreign countries. So, the meaning they read into alien was different, distinct and opposed to, not foreign. This use of alien varied and occurred. For example, it was used 18 times in relation to Ireland in 1885, 3 times in relation to Ireland and 20 times in relation to Wales (on the issue of the Established Church (Wales) Bill) in 1895, and 1 time in relation to Ireland in 1905.

While alien was used in parts of Britain to distinguish people from other parts of the United Kingdom, in 1841 the application of alien instead of foreigner or stranger mainly encompassed people from other countries or in general subjects of a foreign state, including those who resided in the United Kingdom.[17] However, over the years to 1921 the spotlight of public attention on aliens would often focus on specific nationalities or groups. One of the first articles after 1841 in *The Times* on an individual alien concerned a native from Tuscany (later part of Italy),[18] but the first group to become an outstanding subject of public attention consisted of French nationals. The earlier mentioned Alien Act of 1793 and other legislation on aliens passed during the Napoleonic Wars were mostly, if not specifically, aimed at French citizens in or coming to Britain. In 1848, they and other refugees from the revolutionary turmoil in continental Europe were again the main subjects of an Alien Act.[19] In that year the numerical use of alien rose, fuelled by increased debate as the proposed law met opposition, which was followed by further growth the next year, mostly in the numerous reports on discussions about these foreigners.

These debates continued at the end of the 1850s but were increasingly conducted with a sinister undertone as a result of several murder trials. The first case concerned Maria or Marie de Roux, born in French-speaking Lausanne, Switzerland. She worked as a domestic servant and had married British-born Frederick Manning. In 1849 the couple stood trial for the murder of Patrick O'Connor, possibly Maria's lover. The case was reported as the 'Bermondsey Horror' – in this London neighbourhood Manning had allegedly first shot O'Connor with a pistol and then killed his victim by striking him on the back of the head with a crowbar. Maria was indicted for being present, aiding and abetting Manning to commit the felony. Her lawyer argued that as an alien she was entitled to a trial by a jury consisting of aliens, but the court rejected this argument as Maria was married to a British-born man and was therefore no longer regarded as an alien.[20] The couple were convicted and hanged outside Horsemonger Lane Gaol in London. The novelist Charles Dickens attended the execution, and opposing capital punishment in public and giving the case wider exposure, he wrote in a letter to *The Times*: 'I believe that a sight so inconceivably awful as the wickedness and levity of the immense crowd collected at that execution this morning could be imagined by no man, and could be presented in no heathen land under the sun.' And: 'The horrors of the gibbet and of the crime which brought the wretched murderers to it.' The crowd had revelled throughout the night before the execution 'yelling in strong chorus of parodies on Negro melodies with substitutions of "Mrs. Manning" for "Susannah"'.[21]

Another notorious alien to stand trial for murder was Emmanuel Barthélemy, a French revolutionary who opposed the reign of King Louis-Phillipe I. In

1839 Barthélemy was beaten by a policeman during a public protest in France. Five weeks later he shot a police officer. Following time in forced labour, Barthélemy took part in the June 1848 insurrection, was arrested again and imprisoned, but escaped and fled to London. In the British capital he was said to have plotted to return to France and assassinate Napoleon III (the former president of France who was emperor from 1852 to 1870).[22] Barthélemy was also suspected of murdering sodawater-maker George Moore in London's Warren Street in 1854. Moore was allegedly beaten with a stick, then shot and killed. A neighbouring greengrocer, who had heard the commotion, saw Barthélemy leaving Moore's house. The grocer attempted to stop Barthélemy but was shot and fatally wounded by the Frenchman, who was apprehended by a bystander after a chase and a violent struggle. Barthélemy was tried in London, found guilty for the murder of the greengrocer and sentenced to death.[23]

A plot to kill Napoleon III also figured in a third trial. This time the accused was Simon Bernard. He was named as a fellow conspirator of Felice Orsini. In 1858 Orsini and his accomplices threw three bombs at a carriage taking Napoleon III to the opera. The emperor was unhurt, but 8 people were killed and 142 wounded. Orsini was arrested the next day. The bombs were said to have been made in Britain, where Bernard had lived in exile for several years. He was tracked down and tried. The trials of the alleged plotters in Paris and Bernard in London were widely reported and discussed, in *The Times* sometimes under the same heading: 'The late attempt to assassinate the French Emperor'.[24]

Bernard's alien status was brought up at an initial police court hearing by the counsel for the Crown, who argued that British subjects could be tried in Britain for murder committed abroad, and 'an alien whose sovereign was in amity with the Crown of England owes local allegiance with this country while he resided in it. Thus, a foreigner living in England was subject to English law, and differed in no respect from a native in his obligations thereto.'[25] Bernard's lawyer protested but did not pursue this matter.[26] The idea resurfaced at the eventual trial when Bernard was asked whether he wanted to 'exercise his privilege of being tried by [a jury consisting] half [of] aliens and half [of] Englishmen', and answered: 'I trust with confidence to a jury of Englishmen.'[27] Following a six-day trial he was acquitted.[28]

Despite Bernard being found not guilty, this case and the two earlier trials associated aliens in the public mind with murder and political assassination. In 1858 the use of alien in *The Times* reached its highest number in the period 1841–60 in total, and in 14 of these instances the alien was a foreigner in Britain who was involved in political crime and revolutionary violence. This helped to give rise to the idea that some forms of violence could not be committed by Englishmen but only by aliens, an opinion that grew in strength as the century progressed, was extended from French to other foreigners and endured well into the twentieth century.[29]

A later example shows another group of aliens being tarred with that brush. Following the third murder of which Jack the Ripper was suspected, a local London paper reported under the heading 'A Riot against the Jews' as follows:

> On Saturday in several quarters of East London the crowds who assembled in the streets began to assume a very threatening attitude towards the Hebrew population of the District. It was repeatedly asserted that no Englishman could have perpetrated such a horrible crime as that of Hanbury Street, and that it must have been done by a JEW – and forthwith the crowds began to threaten and abuse such of the unfortunate Hebrews as they found in the streets.[30]

The word alien had already other but as yet unrelated associations. In 1844 a leader article in *The Times* offered a different use of alien, denoting a social underclass that was an enemy to society. The paper sought to promote initiatives and interventions to break down the walls between rich and poor in '[great] cities [that] cannot be left alone in the same way as rural districts'. It argued that the mushrooming British cities were attracting the strong and noble, but as the great sinks of the nation, they also drew all that was weak and vile, spreading poverty and vice, and creating misery and degradation – 'the growth of an alien and ungovernable race in strongholds of darkness'.[31] The paper concluded that this alien race posed a threat to British civilisation.

Alien had acquired more connotations. The earlier mentioned rejected elector was said to be in 'want of an occupation', meaning he was poor, a label that in this period was already attached to aliens in Britain in general.[32] As will be discussed, later it stuck even more firmly to aliens. Furthermore, the reporter of the case stated that the elector 'could hardly speak English intelligibly' and indicated that he was a Jew – 'the court was crowded by members of the Jewish nation'[33] – invoking the connotation of an alien being a Jew and possibly a perjurer, who was unable to speak English. The newspaper returned to the theme of Jewish aliens on the eve of the parliamentary debate on Jewish access to full civil rights in 1847.[34] Jews were easily marked as aliens,[35] and these reports helped to set the tone for later years. Sometimes this connotation would be combined with other general prejudice and specific perceptions of Jews. For example, *The Times* later published a letter about Rumanian Jews becoming a threat to civilised society and the paper reported a trial in the Thames Police Court against 'alien intruders' who were found guilty of melting down currency, echoing medieval accusations of Jewish coin clipping.[36]

1861–80

Apart from 1864, between 1861 and 1880 the use of alien in *The Times* was annually higher than the yearly average of the preceding two decennia (Table 10). This was mostly a result of its application as an adjective meaning foreign and a noun meaning foreigner. Apart from 1867 and 1875 this mainly related to people outside Britain. Other outstanding years in this period were 1868 and 1869. From 1875 the use of alien more than doubled and almost tripled in 1880 when compared to 1841. Also notable is that 1867 saw a significant rise in the use of alien as an adjective, meaning different, distinct and opposed to,[37] which climbed to an unprecedented height the next year and then declined somewhat but remained relatively high.

A major source in this period for the use of alien in *The Times*, especially in the early years, was foreign news reporting, such as correspondence on the American Civil War (1861–65) and conflicts in the Balkans and Asia. Alien was also used frequently in reports on foreign countries and part of the British Empire such as India. However, on two occasions home affairs news shed light on aliens in Britain. In 1864 a young German tailor, Franz Müller, was tried and hanged for the murder of Thomas Briggs. The case caught the public eye, as Briggs was killed on a train, a novelty on this still modern form of transport. What also spoke to people's imagination was that Scotland Yard had to pursue Müller across the Atlantic Ocean and caught him in New York, while the defendant's alien status was discussed in court.[38]

The second occasion involved not a criminal but the ironmaster Bernhard Samuelson. He was born in Hamburg. His father, who became a merchant in Liverpool, had been born in Petersburg, Virginia (United States), and his grandfather was a London resident. Samuelson had worked in engineering and manufacturing before he bought a factory in Banbury. Here he became a successful businessman. Samuelson represented the town in parliament in 1859 but lost his seat in the same year. In 1865 he was elected again as MP for Banbury. This time his defeated opponent petitioned against him on the grounds that Samuelson was an alien. The petition was rejected, because according to *The Times*, Samuelson, 'being the grandson of a person actually born on British territory, was capable of being fully naturalized and acquiring all the rights of an Englishman'. The paper congratulated Samuelson, but voiced unease about the legislation that enabled Samuelson to sit in parliament: 'the rights of citizenship in a country ought to depend on the alien's own acts, and not on the accidents of an ancestor's birth. If a man spent a number of years in this country […] it would be fair to give him [these] rights.'[39]

The same article in *The Times* noted that the law which allowed Samuelson to sit in parliament would also 'admit a great part of the population of the United States'. However, the paper had other issues with Americans in the United Kingdom, namely concerns about their influence in the Fenian movement.[40] The expression of these concerns contributed to the spike in the use of alien in 1867.

The Fenian Brotherhood had been founded in 1858 by Irish republicans in the United States, and it was followed by a counterpart in the United Kingdom, the Irish Republican Brotherhood. In March 1867 they launched an armed uprising in Ireland. However, it was badly organised and failed. As part of the chaotic plans, a ship with a few dozen Fenians sailed from the United States to the Irish west coast, where she landed her passengers, who mainly made for Cork. Like other members of the Fenian leadership, they were arrested and convicted. In April 1867, the case of 'Captain John M'Cafferty' was heard in Dublin. He was suspected of having planned an attack on Chester Castle in England on the eve of the insurrection, to ransack it for arms and ammunition, tear up a railway line, cut telegraph cables and capture a mail steamer to carry the weapons and munition to Ireland. The attorney general stated that 'the prisoner was an alien, a native of Ohio, in the United States. He had been tried and acquitted in Cork on a point of law.'[41] However, according to the Crown, M'Cafferty could stand trial for treason. The judges agreed and M'Cafferty was convicted.[42]

Other Fenian leaders escaped, some fled to England and their eventual arrest brought terrorism for the first time to Britain. Two Fenians were arrested in Manchester, but the police van in which they were transported was intercepted by republicans and the two men were freed. A police sergeant was shot dead during the escape. Meanwhile, in London two other Fenians were incarcerated in Clerkenwell Prison. An attempt was made to free them by blowing a hole in the prison wall, but the bomb failed to explode. The Fenians tried again the next day, demolishing a large section of the wall, but no one escaped, while the blast damaged several nearby houses, killing 12 people. The suspects of the 'Clerkenwell Outrage'[43] were tried in April 1868.

There appeared to be numerous Americans among the Fenians. As they were regarded as aliens, the republican rebellion associated aliens not only with political crime and revolutionary violence, a perception that had affected French exiles earlier, but also with the phenomenon of modern terrorism. Terrorism was not new, the 1605 Gunpowder Plot can be called an act of terrorism, but in the middle of the nineteenth century it was newly associated with groups such as the Fenians and the novel use of high explosives such as dynamite.

The Fenian activity also fuelled the debate about Ireland, which brought about the Home Government Association in 1870 and the Home Rule League three years later. The reports in *The Times* on the Fenian rebellion and the following debate regularly quoted Irish politicians who were keen to apply the word alien to distinguish Ireland from Britain, which contributed to the rise in 1867 and 1868 in the use of alien as an adjective, meaning different, distinct and opposed to.[44] The hike in the use of alien as a noun meaning foreigner in 1875 was a result of reports on a Tipperary election with the candidate being declared 'a statutory alien, and therefore disqualified' as he was a United States citizen.[45]

Apart from reaffirming the idea that aliens were responsible for extreme violence and creating the new connotation of terrorism, this period further strengthened two existing feelings often expressed about aliens, namely that they were poor and that they could be Jewish, while it brought the East End of London to the attention of the readers of *The Times*. In 1867 a letter-writer directed them to 'a national calamity'. He had witnessed distress in the Poplar district of the capital's East End. More than a thousand men, five times the usual number, had been seen breaking hard stones in a cold and muddy yard of the parish workhouse. Almost 10,000 persons in the district were receiving parochial and charitable assistance – if Limehouse, Shadwell and Stepney were added, 27,000 were said to depend on aid. Consumption (tuberculosis) was reportedly on the rise. The author of the letter sought the causes of distress first in international market problems, factory closures, the economic crash of the previous year and price rises caused by trade union wage demands. The letter then noted how the earlier prosperity had attracted newcomers to the East End: 'This alien population – not easy to move and impossible to employ – now shares the starvation of the natives, and adds formidably to the [...] burden of the parish.'[46] Without laying the blame for destitution on the aliens, apart from mentioning their immobility and unemployability, this letter was an early publication of a claim that immigration increased East End problems such as poverty and job shortages at a time of economic crisis.[47] The economic crash mentioned by the letter writer was followed in 1873 by a long-term recession, which became known as the 'Great Depression'. It was in the public discourse and political debates that centred on this depression that immigrants were blamed for East End problems.

London's East End was traditionally an area where many immigrants settled.[48] It had attracted French Protestant Huguenot refugees in the seventeenth century and Irish migrants in the eighteenth. While the capital as a whole pulled in people from all over Britain, foreign newcomers often settled near the Thames alongside merchant ship crews that were paid off at the end of their voyage and waiting for new employment. Among them were Lascars from South East Asia as well as African and Chinese men. The indigent black population also contained former slaves from Caribbean and North American plantations.

It did not escape public attention that the immigrant population contained many Jews. By making reference to 'the German Israelite community'[49] to which the grandfather of the earlier-mentioned Bernhard Samuelson had belonged, *The Times* in 1866 identified him as a Jew. The newspaper may not have intended to set him apart for this reason and it usually did not display anti-Jewishness. In fact, *The Times* was alarmed about a new phenomenon in Germany that it reported in 1880, namely 'anti-Semitism' or the organised hatred of Jews. It was a sign of the times that these reports repeatedly declared that Jews formed an 'alien race'.[50]

However, in this period the word race was often used in a different sense than its modern meaning, and was similarly attached to national, foreign and colonial populations to distinguish them from the 'Anglo-Saxon race'.[51] Many publications in the United Kingdom used the word race to differentiate people from specific areas of the kingdom, such as West Britons – the Irish – and North Britons – the Scots. It was not until later that the concept of race dominated fears about national identity, genetically determined group characteristics and physical degeneration caused by unwanted aliens. These fears were voiced by respectable men, including MPs. James Lowther suggested 'the best Blood of the country' was emigrating, Howard Vincent said that 'people emigrated from the United Kingdom last year, their places were taken by [...] the scum of Europe' and Harry Lawson stated 'this unrestricted flow will be likely to weaken and vitiate the whole stream of our national life'. Such feelings were not restricted to Conservative politicians but shared by men such as the Fabian Socialist Sidney Webb.[52]

1881–90

The decennium 1881–90 saw a further rise in the use of alien, meaning distinct, different and opposed to and foreign(er) and strange(r), but what was remarkable about the use of the second meaning in *The Times* was that the paper now increasingly wrote about aliens who lived in Britain (Table 10). These aliens were occasionally referred to as Jewish, German and Italian immigrants, but a later report also mentioned other foreigners, such as an 'alien beggar' who had the French nationality.[53] Another report covering the destination of immigrants who had arrived in the United Kingdom distinguished

Italians, Dutchmen and Belgians. The reporter joked about hundreds of the Italians who had gone to Wales 'which is probably explained by the liking of the youth of the Principality for ice-cream'.[54]

This quip brings out a positive connotation of alien. Favourable associations of the word have not yet been discussed in this book, which does not suggest they did not exist. French, German and Dutch immigrants were acknowledged for bringing technological knowledge to key areas of trade and commerce, such as textile production, mining and metalworking. One of them, Lewis Heymann, who had come from Germany and settled in Nottingham in 1834 to establish the lace firm Heymann & Alexander, became a prominent local politician. In 1857, already an alderman, he was elected mayor of the Borough of Nottingham, and thus became the town's first foreign-born municipal leader. His son became a councillor and deputy lieutenant of Nottinghamshire. Meanwhile, Russians, Poles and Lithuanians were complimented for supplying highly demanded labour to British industries and were praised as being 'industrious' and 'frugal' workers.[55] British taste buds were also knowingly partial to some foreign flavours, such as those contained in the products of German pork butchers, sugar bakers and beer brewers. Italians and Germans were seen to enrich people's lives with art, such as their musical compositions and performances, from grand symphonies to choral singing.[56] However, these favourable opinions were drowned in waves of negative comment at a time of a relatively large influx of immigrants, returning economic problems that affected many workers who formed a growing audience for politicians seeking election, and new ideas about race and identity such as eugenics.

Usually in this period *The Times* did not give a country of origin when it used the word alien, writing, for example, about aliens in Britain in general. Much of this use appeared in 1882 reports on a new Prevention of Crime (Ireland) Bill. In May 1882, the newly appointed chief secretary for Ireland, Lord Frederick Cavendish, was murdered. Only hours after his arrival in Dublin and taking the oath at Dublin Castle, Cavendish, walking in Phoenix Park with Thomas Burke, the permanent under-secretary, was attacked by knife-carrying Irish nationalists, who killed the two men. A few days later in parliament, the killings were called 'the first political assassinations in our century', labelled as 'outrages' and said to be part of 'a reign of terror', which made special measures necessary.[57] In an echo from the Fenian troubles, aliens such as United States citizens of Irish ancestry were suspected to be among the terrorists, their accomplices and supporters, and it was proposed to enable their arrest and deportation.[58]

An editorial in *The Times* returned to this issue in 1884 with a piece called 'Alien laws'. It related 'dynamite outrages, so numerous this year' and perpetrated by foreigners, and asked whether the government should have the power to supervise aliens and expel those who were found to be of suspicious character. The article compared England to other European countries, stating it was the only country without powers to check on foreigners within its borders. A comparison was made with France, where foreigners without visible means of subsistence could be deported, and Belgium, where foreign political agitators were expelled. The author wrote about previous alien legislation, but on the present situation he applied a phrase which would return with a vengeance in later debates: 'the hordes [...] who were invading the country'. He also mentioned the case in England of a German who was serving time for burglaries, but would be discharged when he completed his sentence and 'turned loose into London'.[59] The paper felt that laws were needed to control not only alien terrorists but also criminals as well as vagabonds and exiled politicians. However, the article warned that new legislation would require a change in English manners and customs, which demanded that people kept their nose out of other people's business. A law to register and supervise aliens, *The Times* stated, could only be operative when retailers and landlords helped to enforce it by spying on their customers and tenants and reporting suspicious behaviour to the authorities.

Articles on alien crime mostly covered trials in London, but alien suspects were found across the country. In Nottingham, for example, three aliens were accused of robbing tills, and stealing 80 shillings from a tobacconist and stationer. Sometimes it concerned very petty crime. For instance, Yarmouth Police Court heard on one occasion that an Italian sweet and ice-cream seller, his 15-year-old son and two others were charged with stealing fowl.[60]

In addition, this period brought an expression of a connotation of aliens with vice, and from this time foreigners and immoral behaviour could be closely connected. In 1886 the Austro-Hungarian Club in London's Marlborough Street became subject of a memorial of inhabitants of the neighbourhood, who complained about the nuisance caused by dancing and music that was carried on throughout the night in the club and the disorderly conduct of members outside it. The complaint caused a police raid, which met opposition from the doormen, who fought for minutes with the officers, unsuccessfully trying to prevent them from searching the establishment. The raid resulted in charges against the club's manager and its secretary, a man with the German-sounding name Frederick Koch. It was alleged that the 'place was notoriously the resort of bad characters, 995 women having been seen to enter the club during one month'. The police inspector who searched the building revealed who these women were when he stated that he had found 'several gentlemen and prostitutes, all of them more or less excited with drink'.[61]

The growing number of immigrants in Britain, which rose quicker during this period than before, notably in England (Table 1), may have caused some of the increased use of alien. However, for contemporaries it was difficult to assess figures on immigration, for example, because it was impossible to tell transmigrants apart from settlers. The numbers that were circulated remained opaque, notably in the periods between the publication of census reports. Other sources sometimes produced staggering figures. On one occasion a minister from Edinburgh told a Glasgow meeting that 5,428 Jews had travelled to Scotland from Russia during the previous year, saying that in the week preceding the meeting 105 people had arrived.[62] It was also claimed that in Tower Hamlets in the East End of London, the Conservatives had objected to no less than 1,400 elector applications from people because they were said to be aliens.[63]

Figures like this prompted the secretary of the Board of Trade, Henry Calcraft, to submit a memorandum to parliament in 1887 and explain that as census figures were available only to 1881, politicians could seek more information from the more up-to-date statistics kept by the Board. He warned that the Board tables were far from complete.[64] Although incomplete and often disputed,[65] the Board information on the number of foreign passengers arriving in Britain would soon play a role in the widespread perception that a great number of aliens were arriving and settling in the country.

Less than two weeks after the Calcraft memorandum a journalist called Arnold White wrote a letter to *The Times* about 'the invasion of London by pauper foreigners'. He claimed that the arrival of Jewish immigrants from Russia and Poland caused the 'complete saturation of certain trades with cheap labour' which forced English people out of jobs and deteriorated working conditions for all.[66] A frequently used contemporary term was 'sweating' – a system of subcontracting in some trades, which often caused people on low wages to labour for long hours in poor conditions and small, unsanitary workshops. Immigrants were associated with sweating. White also felt immigration had resulted in overcrowding and high rents, which pushed the English-born population out of neighbourhoods such as Whitechapel.

White was one of the early agitators against alien immigration. Whatever his motives may have been – he possibly wished to improve general working and living conditions[67] – White poisoned the public debate on aliens through the words he used, such as 'invasion' and 'paupers', culminating in his quote from Edmund Burke's 1783 speech on the East India Bill, which was reproduced out of context in the 1887 letter: 'They roll in one after another, wave after wave, and there is nothing before the eyes of the natives but an endless, hopeless prospect of new flights of birds of prey and of passage, with appetites continually renewing for a food that is continually wasting.'[68]

The heading above the letter was 'Pauper Foreigners'. Three years later White wrote another letter, which appeared under the heading 'The Invasion of Pauper Aliens'.[69]

Later the *Daily Mail* described this invasion, setting the scene at the docks of London: 'a huge vessel of [...] gargantuan proportions [...] No sooner is she made fast than out of her bowels swarms a horde of dirty, half-starved, evil-smelling immigrants – Poles, Russians, Germans, Italians, every nationality under the sun [covering] the dock as a cloud of locusts [on] a field of green corn.'[70] Earlier, the *East London Advertiser* had conjured up an image of a large, dense group coming to the capital: 'The swarm of foreign Jews, who have invaded the London East End'.[71] And it further raised the alarm with: 'Notwithstanding all the outcry about the immigration of foreign paupers the cry is "Still they Come".'[72]

White was not alone. The Conservative MP John Colomb (Tower Hamlets Bow & Bromley) spoke about restriction of immigration in 1887 when he asked the secretary of the Board of Trade what steps had been taken to collect information on foreign labour in East London and requested the approximate number of 'destitute'[73] immigrants in the previous five years. When he was unhappy with the answer, the MP inquired: 'What great States of the World, other than Great Britain, permit the immigration of destitute aliens without restriction' and was the government 'prevented [...] from making such regulations as shall put a stop to the free import of destitute aliens into the United Kingdom?'[74]

It was not the first time Colomb had spoken in parliament on this subject. In 1886 he had asked about foreign competition in the labour market.[75] He returned to this issue in March 1887, wondering how many 'persons during the past year have been sent back to the United Kingdom from the United States, and from other countries, by reason of their being destitute aliens'.[76] Half a year later Colomb mentioned the cases of 'nine persons, said to be foreigners, who, with others, have been recently sent back to the United Kingdom by the United States as destitute aliens'.[77] In 1890, Colomb spoke twice in parliament about destitute foreigners and immigrants, including an Italian family,[78] but he did not mention the subject again, speaking later mostly about naval and military issues. The words and phrases he used in parliament sounded rather moderate, but outside Westminster he did not mince his words. In 1888 Colomb told the *East End News*: 'I object to England with its overcrowded population, being made a human ashpit for the refuse population of the world.'[79]

As the Westminster parliament discussed immigration, in 1887 the government sent its representatives in Europe and the United States a dispatch requesting copies of any laws or local regulations 'prohibiting the admission or continued residence of destitute aliens'.[80] During the same year the Home Office received a deputation led by White protesting against increased immigration in the United Kingdom. White recommended following the United States example of restrictive legislation.[81] An 1888 Select Committee also inquired into United States laws, notably on pauper and destitute aliens. A few years later the Foreign Office made a similar enquiry, focusing on the expulsion of aliens.

A collaborator of White and another – though slightly later – correspondent in *The Times* was William Wilkins, a writer who used the pseudonym W. H. de Winton.[82] Wilkins was for a while private secretary of Windham Thomas Wyndham-Quin, the fourth Earl of Dunraven, a journalist and Conservative politician who served briefly as under-secretary of state for the Colonies. Following an unsuccessful attempt in the form of the Society for the Suppression of Destitute Aliens, in 1891 Dunraven and White set up the equally short-lived Association for Preventing the Immigration of Destitute Aliens. Wilkins acted as its secretary. Proposals of Dunraven for restricting immigration were written up by Wilkins in *The Alien Invasion* (1892), published in the 'Social Questions of Today' series. During the same year Dunraven published the article 'The invasion of destitute aliens' in *The Nineteenth Century* magazine.[83] Wilkins also contributed to White's anthology *The Destitute Alien in Great Britain: A Series of Papers Dealing with the Subject of Foreign Pauper Immigration*, published in 1892.[84]

As Fishman has pointed out, more radical and left-wing individuals shared some of these anti-alien feelings. He has, for example, referred to the novelist John Law, the pen name of Margaret Harkness, a Socialist and feminist. In Law's *Out of Work* (1888), a radical carpenter vents his spleen on foreign furriers: 'They'll go to hell.' His wife echoes: 'Why should they come here I'd like to know? London ain't what it used to be; it's just like a foreign city. The food ain't English; the talk ain't English. Why should all them foreigners come here to take our food out of our mouths, and live on victuals we wouldn't give to pigs?' And a politically conscious female radical labour master forcibly maintains: 'No, I never take on a foreigner. It's bad enough for us English and I won't help to make it worse by giving work to a Jewess!'[85]

It can of course be questioned whether Harkness herself held such beliefs or was merely describing typical people and their views. In any case, as a result of the expression of such feelings and wider anti-alien and sweating agitation, parliament appointed two committees: a House of Commons Select Committee; and a House of Lords Select Committee.[86] The newspaper articles on their meetings and reports contributed to the rising use of the word alien in these years.

1891–1910

The sharper rise in the use of alien in *The Times*, meaning foreign(er) and strange(r) and foreigner and stranger in Britain, was after 1891 accompanied by a slow decline in the use of alien meaning distinct, different and opposed to (Table 10). It seems as if the increased use of alien for describing foreigners and strangers in Britain made it harder for journalists to use the word as an adjective in the general sense of something or someone being different.[87]

An increased use of alien as a synonym for foreigner or stranger occurred in reports on parliamentary debate and legislation. The discussions were often prompted by questions whether the government intended to exclude immigrants, notably from Germany and Russia. *The Times* reported that the 'uniform answer was that there was no need to take extreme measures'.[88] Supporters and opponents of restriction on alien immigration used the Board of Trade figures mentioned by Henry Calcraft in 1887. Sometimes these figures were alarming, sometimes they were reassuring. For example, showing that in July 1891 a total of 4,956 aliens arrived in ports across the kingdom who stated that they were not on their way to America. In addition, 13,953 aliens arrived and stated they were bound for America. In comparison, during the same month in 1890 the figures were, respectively, 3,761 not going to America and 9,141 bound for America, and for the first seven months of 1891 they amounted to 20,866 and 62,174 – averaging less than 3,000 and 9,000 per month. These figures were published but called 'imperfect' in *The Times*. In some ports only deck passengers and people who proceeded by train as third-class passengers were counted. Nevertheless, the paper felt that 'they go far to refute some exaggerated ideas' on alien immigration. It stated: 'The danger lies in the future [...] In a little time emigration [from Germany and Eastern Europe] becomes organized and systematic without the concert of Governments, and perhaps against their wishes, and then there is no limit to the magnitude of the stream.' However, *The Times* saw as yet no need for strong measures such as refusing pauper aliens to land, but it felt 'the matter requires watching, and something might be done to lessen the stream and prevent its becoming a river, without abandoning the traditional hospitality of Great Britain towards foreigners'.[89]

With these words *The Times* in 1891 framed the debate on alien immigration for the next 15 years. That discussion continued as there was no let-up in newspaper reports on aliens with some by-now familiar and with some new connotations. They caused overcrowding, were destitute, proved dangerously fraudulent,[90] stole jobs and brought diseases such as cholera and trachoma.[91] In 1893, 1894 and in 1895 White wrote again to *The Times* about the 'foreign paupers' and 'undesirable aliens'.[92] He used the label undesirable first in 1894.

In that year the Conservative former prime minister but now leader of the opposition, Lord Salisbury (Robert Gascoyne-Cecil), introduced an alien bill. His proposal had two elements. First, restriction of immigration of pauper and therefore undesirable aliens, because of the burden of their upkeep and their threat to the jobs of native workers. Second, a proposal to give the government the power to expel aliens suspected of crime, including political violence. *The Times* doubted whether there was an open 'welcome for paupers' door that had be closed, but the paper was in no doubt about the desirability to keep violent political criminals away.[93] Nevertheless, the bill was rejected by the Liberals. A subsequent bill failed similarly after being proposed in 1898 by Albert Yorke, the sixth Earl of Hardwicke and later under-secretary of state for India and under-secretary of state for war.[94]

The call for restriction of alien immigration continued. The main arguments of the opponents of restriction centred on the benefits of a free international market with open borders and the desirability of maintaining Britain as a safe haven or asylum for refugees and persons who suffered religious and political oppression abroad. In 1901, *The Times* wrote: 'the pauper alien has got on the nerves of many persons',[95] but the paper tried to offer a balanced view. It stated aliens had been blamed for lowering wages and standards of living but argued that official documents had shown this to be an exaggeration, as were the reports about high numbers of immigrants. Later the paper voiced a similar opinion, but it did not dismiss proposals for steps that could be taken to restrict immigration of 'undesirable' aliens, although it questioned whether such measures could be implemented successfully.[96]

As meetings were conducted in the East End to protest about immigrants causing problems, a parliamentary committee on regulation of alien immigration was formed in 1901. It boasted a membership of 69 MPs.[97] The next year it was followed by a Royal Commission, which was announced as news reports continued to link aliens to poverty, disease, overcrowding and petty crime as well as gambling and illegal distilling. It was to 'inquire and report on the character and extent of the evils which are attributed to the unrestricted immigration of aliens, especially in the metropolis, and the measures which have been adopted for the restriction and control of alien immigration in foreign countries and in British colonies'.[98] The Commission's report and recommendations led to the formulation of an Aliens Bill, which fell at the committee stage, because of what supporters of the bill, including Howard Vincent, called the 'obstruction'[99] of the opponents of restriction in committee discussions. A new bill was introduced, resulting after much debate in the Aliens Act of 1905, which came into force in 1906.

As the remit of the Royal Commission showed, the alien legislation in the United Kingdom was influenced by measures taken abroad. Immigration control was a worldwide phenomenon, notably the half century from 1880 was a period of growing restriction. Prussia, for example, one of the leading states in the German Empire, had earlier established and was maintaining a tightly regulated regime.[100] Another major power, France, had the already mentioned regulations to deal with what the French authorities regarded as undesirable immigrants. Smaller countries followed. For example, as stated above, Belgium developed an immigration policy.[101] The *Daily Mail* wrote in 1897 about other countries, such as Austria, Russia, Greece, Switzerland and Sweden, which had erected obstacles to foreigners entering specific professions and thrown up hurdles to naturalisation of immigrants.

Similar measures had already or were being taken in the British Empire, and they too affected the debate in Britain.[102] As Basford and Gilchrist have shown,[103] from 1880s states that had arisen from British colonies and self-governing British colonies in America, Australia and Africa began introducing laws to regulate the entry of immigrants. These measures were discussed in Britain. For example, Montague Crackanthorpe referred to the colonies in his contribution to Arnold White's 1892 anthology *The Destitute Alien in Great Britain*. During the same year the UK Board of Trade commissioned a report on the laws relating to immigration of foreigners into the United States. And W. H. Wilkins, in his 1892 book *The Alien Invasion*, referred to undesirable aliens in America.

In general, the new legislation in English-speaking British colonies and former colonies, such as the United States, which preceded the 1905 Aliens Act, was often based on existing powers to regulate immigration, which had been enforced since the 1850s. Specifically, colonial and former colony jurisdictions had legislated and continued to legislate to restrict the arrival and settlement of Asian people. The government in London was not simply a bystander. Bashford and McAdam have written: 'When various self-governing colonies within the British Empire sought to mention Chinese, Indians, or Japanese in their immigration statutes, it was the Colonial Office in London that typically tempered such propositions.'[104]

This came into play when some colonies sought immigration restrictions in 1897. London objected against discrimination of people from the British Empire, but Secretary of State Joseph Chamberlain told the Colonial Conference in 1897: 'We quite sympathise with the determination [...] of these colonies [...] that there should not be an influx of people alien in civilisation, alien in religion, alien in customs, whose influx, moreover, would seriously interfere with the legitimate rights of the existing labouring population.'[105] The outcome of the conference was legislation that followed the so-called Natal formula, which was used in the colonies and was neutral on race and nationality, but prescribed a test for prospective immigrants, with persons who failed to write and sign in a European language being prohibited from entering.

The conference thus emulated legislation in South Africa, where the Transvaal Republic had issued the Aliens Expulsion Act in 1896.[106] Using this law the Transvaal government could expel aliens – 'uitlanders' – who were considered to be a danger to the peace and public order. *The Times* reported in January 1897 that while the Transvaal officers had been lenient, the neighbouring Orange Free State had so far only refused entry to four 'penniless' Russian Jews and 'one Chinaman'.[107] However, a month later the colonial secretary was asked in Westminster about 'two Englishmen [who] were recently arrested and deported by the Boer authorities under the Aliens Expulsion Act, and treated with such harshness that one died and the other attempted suicide'.[108] Several months later, an amendment of the Transvaal Aliens Expulsion Act caused the tension with London to rise, inducing the British government to reinforce troops in South Africa. Tensions escalated again in the late 1890s. When no compromise could be reached, the position of English immigrants in the Afrikaner republics became one of the disputed issues leading to the Second South African War.[109]

How the South African legislation and war influenced the debate in Britain arises from the testimony of White, which he gave to the Royal Commission on Alien Immigration in 1902: 'For six years after 1884 he had paid annual visits to South Africa for the purpose of planting small colonies of English labourers and artisans.' The absurdity of replacing them in England with 'foreigners of doubtful value' had then sprung upon his mind. The crux of the problem 'was primarily racial', which for White explained the willingness of the aliens to perform cheap labour and live in overcrowded houses. White also objected to alien immigration 'on the ground of the pro-Boerism – their anti-nationalism to [the United Kingdom], the evidence as to which was perfectly clear to his mind'.[110] Although perhaps not directly an outcome of White's testimony, the Commission's recommendations and later the Aliens Act of 1905 followed examples of foreign and colonial legislation, for instance, on classifications of undesirable aliens, which included prostitutes and persons living on the proceeds of prostitution.

However, despite the legislation in (former) parts of the empire exerting influence in London, there were remarkable differences between United States and colonial laws on one side and the United Kingdom Aliens Act of 1905 on the other. A disparity was the exemption made in the United Kingdom for people who were religiously and politically persecuted – the right of asylum. A majority of British politicians held onto the idea of their country being a safe haven for those in need. In addition, British legislation did not have an outspoken ethnic character and, as it did not divide people according to what was regarded as their race, the Aliens Act of 1905 was dissimilar.

A further difference can be found in the name of the 1905 Act. The Royal Commission on Alien Immigration concluded that one of the most important elements of the colonial laws was that they made no distinction among the immigrants between aliens and British subjects. The Commission did not want to exclude British subjects from across the empire entering the country, because they had an unrestricted right of entry to the United Kingdom: 'We have to observe that the restrictive [colonial] legislation is not directed against Aliens as such [...] The same restriction and prohibitions apply equally to all immigrants. Strictly speaking therefore, there are no laws in the British Colonies restricting Alien Immigration.'[111] Hence, the Commission applied the word alien and its findings contributed to the 'Aliens Act'.

During the debate on the Alien Bills in Britain and following the passing of the 1905 Aliens Act several existing connotations of the word alien acquired a new lease of life.[112] The first undertone that was revitalised with much gusto was about alien involvement in prostitution or 'white slavery' as it was increasingly called.[113] In 1903 Nathan Obstbaum, a 30-year-old jeweller, stood trial and was indicted in London for assaulting and causing actual bodily harm to a young woman, Fredel Birkelvitch. She had arrived from Russian Poland half a year earlier and 'had been forced to go on the streets', but she decided to leave that way of life and tell Obstbaum about her decision. It was alleged that on hearing this news he struck her, 'knocking her down, and giving her a black eye, and while she was on the ground [,] he kicked her more than once, one of the kicks being on the right hip'. The woman was pregnant, delivered of a stillborn child and died of 'septic peritonitis caused by the bursting of an internal abscess'.[114]

Later, *The Times* returned to this issue – the 'white slave traffic' – stating that the enslavers also caught non-alien women: 'The traders in human flesh who decoy English [girls and women] to foreign countries [...] and their victims are not merely physically but morally destroyed.'[115] This coincided with developments in the United States. There in 1903 immigration restrictions had been extended to individuals convicted of felonies, crimes or misdemeanours involving moral turpitude such as prostitution. Seven year later Congress passed the White Slave Traffic Act, which made it a felony to transport women across state borders for the purpose of prostitution, debauchery or any other immoral purpose. The United States example was followed by – unsuccessful – bills introduced in the British parliament. The Conservative MP Arthur Lee, who had been assigned to the British Embassy in Washington, stated in the House of Commons the evils of brothels in their worst form are not so common in this country as abroad: I do not think they are, and I further admit that the particular phase of the white slave traffic in which girls are kidnapped and detained, either by violence or promises or devices of that kind, is not so prevalent in this country as in many others. On the other hand I am afraid it is none the less true that the United Kingdom, and particularly England, is increasingly becoming a clearing-house and depot and dispatch centre of the white slave traffic, and the headquarters of the foreign agents engaged in the most expensive and lucrative phase of the business.[116]

The second connotation to be given new vitality during the Alien Bill debates was that of aliens being Jews. Neither the pimping culprit nor his prostitute victim in the 1903 case, mentioned above, were said to be Jews by *The Times*, but most of its readers must have recognised both of them as such. Later, the newspaper wrote: 'A large part of the organized "white slave trade" is in the hands of Russian and Austrian Jews.'[117] As stated earlier, *The Times* opposed anti-Jewish bias and a statement in the paper by the Jewish author Israel Zangwill that England was 'catching the epidemic that rages everywhere else against the Jew' prompted Prime Minister Arthur Balfour in 1904 to write in a letter to the paper's editor: 'The Aliens Bill is designed to protect the country, not against the Jew, but against the undesirable alien, quite irrespective of his nationality or his creed.'[118] Zangwill replied that the bill was 'inspired by anti-Semites and will reinspire them', and drew Balfour's attention to Jew-baiting in Wales, boycotts in Ireland and pamphleteering in Scotland.[119] Earlier Zangwill had published his novel *Children of the Ghetto* (1892), which told the story of Jewish immigrants in Britain from an insider's perspective and in a sympathetic manner.

Despite Balfour's words, in many minds the Alien Act was a measure against Jewish immigration from Russia. The Royal Commission member Evans-Gordon wrote on the eve of the act coming into force that the problem of the persecution of the Jews in Russia could not be solved by their emigration to the United States and the United Kingdom. The Americans were checking

> the ingress of these people and Great Britain has found it necessary to pass the Aliens Act. It would be a mere calamity if – as is now likely – hosts of poverty-stricken Jews hasten into the East of London and other English ghettos during the few weeks before that Act comes into operation, or are admitted afterwards as political or religious refugees.[120]

However, as stated earlier, the alien label could be attached to all people from other countries. As the already quoted dock scene in the *Daily Mail* made clear, for newspaper journalists aliens included Poles, Russians, Germans, Italians and every other nationality than British. The marker could be applied to groups such as Jews, but it was also attached to others such as gypsies. In 1906 a spate of news about German gypsies contributed to one of the earliest mass deportations of aliens from Britain.[121]

The third connotation that received a new lease of life was the alleged alien threat to native labour. It was brought back into focus in 1906 when attempts were made to amend the Aliens Act on the issue of contract labour and discussions continued about employing alien pilots and seamen such as the Lascars on British ships.[122]

The fourth connotation revived in this period was that of aliens being violent criminals. The issue came up in discussions about the administration of the Aliens Act and its perceived shortcomings, and the debate centred on the restriction of immigration of dangerous aliens and the expulsion of convicted ones. In 1909 the government published a white paper, containing the correspondence between Home Secretary Herbert Gladstone and Judge James Rentoul. The correspondence had started after Rentoul made a speech in February of that year on 'The British Empire: Its Greatness, Glory and Freedom' at the Bishopsgate Institute Hall, in connection with the Guild of Freedom of the City of London. In this speech he reportedly said that he had left the Old Bailey that afternoon, after sitting a week: 'Three of the cases tried were those of the aliens of the very worst kind in their own country.' He added that the number of criminal aliens who had appeared before him had steadily increased over the years, and that the country would be glad to get rid of these people, whom he regarded as a threat to the empire. Rentoul also criticised politicians: 'It was all very well to talk about an open door for the political refugee, [but] men who were known to the police as of bad character should not be allowed to enter the country.'[123] Gladstone replied that actually 21 people had come before Rentoul in that week, of whom 5 were acquitted, and of the 16 who were convicted 3 were aliens. Furthermore, he said that the total number of criminal aliens in England and Wales had decreased from 4,396 in 1904 to 2,665 in 1907. The home secretary added that if a judge declared that a convicted alien ought to be expelled but did not actually recommend this expulsion, the judge was directly responsible for the continued presence of that alien in the country.

Criminal alien violence also figured in the cases of Oscar Slater and Stinie Morrison. *The Times* reported on the Morrison case,[124] but the paper apparently did not pay much attention to Slater. In contrast, the *Glasgow Herald* closely followed his case. As argued elsewhere,[125] the Slater case had a great impact on the general public, notably in Scotland. Slater was a German Jew, who in 1909 was convicted wrongly for the gruesome murder of an elderly Glasgow woman. He was alleged to have been a violent pimp, capable of horrendous crimes, and the trial judge misdirected the jury by saying: '[Slater] has maintained himself by the ruin of men and on the ruin of women, living for many years in a way that many blackguards would scorn to live.'[126] In reaction to Slater's sentence, the influential local magazine *The Bailie* wrote: 'Now an alien breed has come in. Great Britain [...] opens her arms to the foreign scum [...] mole-ish blackguards are on the prowl in the community.'[127] A few days earlier the *Edinburgh Evening News* had written: 'The trial has cast a lurid light on the dark places of our great cities, in which such wretches ply their calling. It shows a brood of alien vampires, lost to conscience, crawling in black depths at the basement of civilised society.'[128]

The fifth connotation that came to life again was that aliens were dangerous terrorists. The correspondence with judge Rentoul, mentioned above, was conducted as Home Secretary Gladstone had to defend the government's wider record on continued immigration, which had come under attack following what was labelled as the 'Tottenham Outrages'. In January 1909 two men armed with pistols robbed messengers from a rubber factory who carried the company's weekly wages. One of the messengers was wounded. The robbery was followed by a spectacular police chase, which lasted several hours and was conducted on foot and by automobile, tramcar and milk van, and during which hundreds of bullets were fired, causing dozens of casualties, including four fatalities – a 10-year-old boy, a police constable and the two robbers. There was immediate speculation about the identity of the criminals, who were variously said to be Indians, Italians, Latvians and Jews. *The Times*, which reported the event as 'an amazing series of outrages, singularly rare if not entirely without parallel in a civilized country',[129] stated the robbers were aliens and members of a revolutionary party, engaged in the manufacture of bombs, which classified them in the public mind as political terrorists. The event was widely reported, with richly illustrated features in the popular press, and attracted much public attention.[130] The funeral procession of the boy and policeman passed along a route lined by hundreds of police officers and a large crowd of several hundred thousand people.

Less than two years later another three policemen were buried in London. In December 1910 police discovered a gang in Hounditch trying to tunnel their way into a jewellery store. However, the thieves got away, killing three unarmed officers and wounding others with automatic pistols. One of the robbers was also injured, died of his wounds and the discovery of his body directed the police to the East End, where in January 1911 a house in Sydney Street was besieged by police and military forces. After shooting from both sides, the house caught fire. Eventually two bodies were found inside. When a wall collapsed fire officers were wounded, one of them fatally.

The Houndsditch murders and siege in Sidney Street caused even more sensation than the Tottenham robbery. Newspaper readers could follow the investigation and street battle in detail, guided by not only traditional drawings but also exciting photographs, for example, a picture in the *Illustrated London News* of two Scots Guards in action.[131] Furthermore, cinema visitors could view a Pathé newsreel, with moving scenes of troop movements on horseback, large crowds, a soldier firing shots, the burning house, the death and wounded being carried away and the Home Secretary Winston Churchill being present at the siege.[132] And there was no doubt about the culprits. In Tottenham, the identity of the criminals was initially a source of speculation. In the Hounditch murders *The Times* immediately reported that an alien had been tracked down and the police attention quickly concentrated on Eastern European and Jewish revolutionaries in Stepney and Whitechapel.[133]

During the first two months of 1911 the use of the word alien in *The Times* was almost always connected to Houndsditch and Sidney Street, and even when unrelated to these events, the use was accompanied by reports on violence and political crime. The paper had already questioned whether aliens could be assimilated into British society and noted the shortcomings of the 1905 Aliens Act – 'undesirable aliens' were still entering the country.[134] The *Daily Mail* presented what it regarded as the 'ordinary man's view', which compared criminal aliens with rats: 'After a hard day's fighting we have exterminated two undesirable aliens. And now what about it?'[135] In a knee-jerk reaction, the government introduced an Aliens (Prevention of Crimes) Bill and the Conservative politician Edward Goulding issued a new Aliens Bill.[136]

Finally, during this period the alien tag was attached to yet another group, namely Chinese immigrants in Britain. It was a small group which fluctuated in size; census figures were inflated as they included Chinese seamen present in Britain on the date of the census (Table 1). In 1891, less than 800 persons born in China were enumerated in Britain, in 1901 there were less than 400 and in 1911 over 1,400, mostly in England and Wales.[137] The Chinese in Britain had been the subject of earlier discussion. For example, in 1888 the *National Review* quoted the Parliamentary Report on Sweating: 'The Chinese, like the Jews, live on next to nothing and work incredibly long hours for incredibly low wages.'[138] This expressed a widely shared contempt for what was regarded as an immoral and 'inferior race'[139] of people with a different skin-colour, physiognomy and language. The disdain was also voiced by Beatrice Potter (the pseudonym of Beatrice Webb): 'The women [of East London] have been fitly termed [...] Chinamen [...] they accept any work at any wage.'[140] The connotation occasionally lay behind the opposition to and violence against the opening of a Chinese laundry or Chinese men signing on as ship's crew. For example, the *Daily Mail* wrote about the Society for the Protection and Advancement of British Industries, which aimed to 'secure abolition of the immigrant Chinaman [...] by refusing to have anything to do with him when he comes'.[141]

Contempt could change to hatred, and towards the end of the nineteenth century a menacing stereotype appeared – 'the Yellow Peril'. At first abroad, as Chinese migrants moved into the United States, Australia, New Zealand and South Africa in larger numbers than in Britain. In 1876, *The Times* had described for its British audience the feeling that underpinned the Page Act in the United States, which was aimed to restrict immigration of, among others, indentured workers from Asia and immoral Chinese women: 'Modern civilization knows no proscription of races [but no race is] more bitterly hated and jealously watched than the Chinese who are pouring down monthly in thousands upon the Pacific coast of the United States.' This hate, wrote the paper, also occurred in Canadian and Australian colonies: 'The resentment of the British immigrant against his Chinese rival rises occasionally to the boiling point.' And according to *The Times*, there was a forecast that in later years would appeal to British sentiments: 'In five years [the people of California] may find themselves matched in numbers – possibly in ten years altogether overpowered – by the rising tide of Mongolian immigration.'[142]

In New Zealand, which had an Aliens Act in 1866 and an Immigration Restriction Act in 1899, immigration from Asia was a major issue. In 1905, the *Daily Mail* wrote about a crime case in Wellington: 'Protest by murder. Why an Englishman shot a Chinaman.' According to the paper, a man called Lionel Terry wanted to warn the New Zealand authorities about Asian immigration. He went to the Chinese quarter in Wellington and 'walked up to an aged Chinaman named Kum Yung, and deliberately murdered him with two shots from a revolver'. The next morning 'Terry, bright and cheerful, went to a bookseller's to inquire about the sale of his book on the yellow peril, "The Shadow". Being told that the sales were not large, he remarked, "It will sell better to-morrow", and he walked to the police station, where he gave himself up as Kum Yung's murderer.' Apparently, Terry had also written to the governor of New Zealand that 'he had decided to bring the matter of alien immigration before the public eye, and to that end had put to death a Chinaman the previous evening'.[143]

The menace in the shape of 'the Yellow Peril' was related to geopolitical developments. Charles H. Pearson referred to the Chinese challenge in his book *National Life and Character: A Forecast* (1893). The phrase possibly originated in the words of the German Emperor Wilhelm II – *die gelbe Gefahr* – to caption an 1897 image by Hermann Knackfuss, called *Völker Europas, wahrt eure heiligsten*

Güter. In the same year *The Spectator* used 'The Yellow Peril' as the heading for an article on a recent German seizure in China.[144] And it appeared in Matthew Phipps Shiel's novel *The Yellow Danger* (1898).

For a while, papers such as the *Daily Mail* reported regularly on 'the Yellow Peril'. However, whether China and Japan really presented a military or economic danger to countries such as Germany, Britain, Russia and the United States was doubtful to contemporaries. Earlier in the nineteenth century China had been a battleground for two Opium Wars, when Britain imposed the drug trade on the Chinese, and the 'Ever Victorious Army' fought against internal rebellions, with European and American officers strengthening the imperial Chinese forces, which were regarded as weak. Eventually, the *Daily Mail* declared the danger a bogey: 'The absurd story that the Chinese and the Japanese were about to make common cause in a kind of holy war of the yellow man against the white races, which has been invented in Germany and circulated by German diplomatic agents for the special purpose of German policy, falls to the ground.'[145]

However, by then the damage was done to public opinion in Britain – the connotation of an alien as a fearsome Chinese immigrant had been made. This coincided with harrowing news about the Boxer uprising in China. In 1897 a band of armed men stormed the residence of a German missionary and killed two priests. In response, the Germans occupied Jiaozhou Bay. This action triggered a scramble for further concessions, as Britain, France, Russia and Japan attempted to secure their own spheres of influence in China, in the words of the *Glasgow Herald*, 'so vast a mass of alien humanity'.[146] Chinese protests against the foreign powers and further attacks on churches followed, culminating in the siege of foreign legacies in Beijing. In a series of sensationalist reports the *Daily Mail* quoted the German emperor under the subheading 'Yellow Peril': 'A crime of unspeakable insolence, horrifying in its barbarity, has been committed against the person of my trusty representative, and has taken him from us. The Ministers of the other Powers hover between life and death, and with them the comrades who were sent for their protection.'[147] The Western actions coincided with looting and atrocities from all sides during the unrest that lasted for several years.

After the British general election of 1906, in which the use of Chinese workers in South African mines – 'coolie labour' – was an issue, the stereotype of 'the Yellow Peril' also got a sexual association. In December 1906 the *Sunday Chronicle* published an article by Claude Blake, called 'Chinese vice in England. A view of terrible conditions at close range'. Blake described how white girls were seduced by Chinese men through drugs and sold as white slaves.[148] The following year *The Times* drew attention to a report by a Liverpool commission of inquiry into Chinese settlements, which may have been Blake's source. According to *The Times* the commission questioned whether the Aliens Act should be strengthened and asked special attention for 'the portion in the report dealing with the relations of Chinamen with white women'.[149] Holmes has also quoted this report, disclosing what lay behind the carefully chosen words of *The Times* as the Liverpool reporters wrote: 'The Chinese appear to much prefer having intercourse with young girls, more especially those of undue precocity.'[150]

These sentiments were re-invoked later by the *Daily Mail* when it repeated the words spoken by a Thames Police Court magistrate, who 'described the problem raised by the relations of Chinamen with white girls as 'a frantic one'. He 'spoke with the fullest knowledge and experience' about half-caste children in several British cities. The same article also mentioned an American commentator who said he would like to see in Britain 'vigorous steps taken by the Government and local authorities to deal with these aliens who decoy white girls'. They should be expelled, and it should be questioned whether mixed marriages were permitted.[151]

1911–20

The even larger rise in the use of alien meaning foreign(er) and strange(r) and foreigner and stranger in Britain in this period (Table 10), related to the First World War and coincided with the overall further but now slow decline in the use of alien meaning of distinct, different and opposed to.

The terms 'German alien' or 'enemy alien' dominated the news about aliens after the United Kingdom entered the war on 4 August 1914. The war also had serious repercussions for foreign nationals residing in Britain, and a devastating effect on some migrant populations. Citizens of enemy states, such as the German, Austro-Hungarian and Turkish empires, suffered verbal abuse and physical attacks and were arrested, registered, interned, black-listed, expelled, deported and repatriated.[152]

However, well before August 1914, popular feelings about aliens had been expressed violently. Three years earlier, in the wake of an unsuccessful miners' strike a wave of violence swept through the western valleys of South Wales. Property – mostly owned by Jewish shopkeepers, pawnbrokers and landlords – was attacked, resulting in the imposition of military rule and evacuation of Jewish families. Although non-Jewish tradesmen were also assaulted and *The Times* wrote that a 'spirit of indiscipline ran riot' with 'bottle-flinging experts' battering 'an alien colony',[153] there was little doubt about the riots being mostly aimed at Jews. Among the rioters were fun-seeking hooligans as well as respectable working people, such as colliers and their wives, who may have feared having to pay debts to traders who had advanced credit.

There was also an element in the South Wales violence of a native population wanting to rid itself of the aliens in its midst.[154] In a not dissimilar situation, again some years earlier, miners in Blantyre, Scotland, said they went on strike against Polish aliens 'until the foreigners are sent away'.[155] And later in Wales a Sunday afternoon riot in Tiger Bay targeted 'Arabs, negroes, and women [in a growing foreign population] after a young girl, daughter of respectable parents, was found in a dazed condition in a doorway, after having been missing for a week'. As with the Chinese, aliens were reported as a threat to young British women, but the wider background to the incident was revealed when a newspaper report suggested that the aliens were to blame for showing off their social and economic successes: '[The] coloured population of Cardiff profited by high wages, almost daily take country rides in motor-cars and carriages, and foreign boarding-house keepers are buying houses in suburbs.'[156]

The 'alien within our gates'[157] became an 'enemy alien' in August 1914, when the Aliens Restriction Act came into force to control the entry, departure, residence and travel of enemy nationals such as Germans, Austro-Hungarians and Turks, who were also compelled to register their presence, usually at police stations. Not all enemy aliens registered, perhaps because they regarded themselves as loyal British citizens. For example, a property owner was fined £50 for failing to register, but ironically the police found a ticket in his pocket, showing he had donated £20 to The Prince of Wales National Distress Fund, an initiative set up to help the families of serving men and those suffering from 'industrial distress'.[158]

Although it was an official term that covered all citizens of countries the United Kingdom was at war with,[159] in public use an enemy alien and even an alien now mostly meant a German, which in itself became a term of abuse. A manager of the Carlton Hotel in Blackpool, a naturalised native from Saxony, sued the *Daily Despatch* in Manchester for reporting about a case, in which he was involved, under a heading 'Alien in possession: The management of a Blackpool hotel'. The paper had also referred to the manager as a German, which he regarded as abusive. The jury awarded the man £50 in damages.[160]

The multitude of reports about war-time events and developments explains the high occurrence of the word alien in *The Times* from 1914 to 1920. The paper's first mention of the term enemy alien was on 1 August 1914, a few days before the Aliens Restriction Act. In the seven months before that date, almost a hundred instances of the use of alien can be found in *The Times*, but none of them associated alien with German, instead they referred to Italians, Jews and other foreigners. As stated earlier, after the outbreak of war alien became a synonym for German. It was also used as a noun to denote Germans and other enemy nationals outside Britain and applied as an adjective for companies, indicating their place of trading, for example, a bank in Germany was called an alien bank, but the Deutsche Bank in London remained a German bank. Newspaper reports continued to use the adjective or noun German, usually mentioning somebody's nationality when they were convicted for offending the alien regulations,[161] but official and judicial documents did not state nationality and used the term enemy alien.

The 1914 Act was followed by measures to arrange the arrest, internment and deportation of aliens. The round-up proceeded awkwardly. In August 1914, local chief constables were instructed to arrest enemy aliens who were suspected of being dangerous. Conversely, some of the arrested men had to be released, because they did not pose a danger or there was nowhere to keep them locked up. The instruction was renewed in October 1914, again followed by releases, until in May 1915 it was decreed that all enemy alien males of military age (17–55) were to be captured for internment. That last order was also issued out of concern for the personal safety of these aliens in a very hostile atmosphere, and at this stage some men surrendered themselves voluntarily for internment. As a result, the total number of civilian German and Austrian prisoners in Britain rose from some 10,000 in September 1914 to about 20,000 in May 1915 and peaked at almost 30,000 in November 1917. The Germans formed the largest group, there were less Austrian internees and the number of Turkish aliens was smaller still. The wives and children of the internees became dependant on the British, German and Austrian governments or had to rely on charity. From the start of the war the policy was to repatriate these women and children as well as older men, but the deportation of the internees and their relatives did not start in earnest until October 1917. Nonetheless, between 1914 and 1919 the number of Germans in the British population was reduced by 58 per cent.

The arrests and internments were mostly aimed at male Germans who were of military age – potential enemy soldiers – but they also had the purpose of preventing espionage. After spy mania had raged through Britain well before the war,[162] in 1914 this issue appealed again to newspaper audiences. Numerous reports were made about German spies. For example, on 6 August 1914 *The Times* reported that the home secretary said he wanted 'to deal with the removal of spies, 21 of whom had been arrested, chiefly in important naval centres, within the preceding 24 hours'. The report listed some of those who were charged. They included a British subject with a German name and a German naval pensioner. Two months later the trial of a suspected German agent, Carl Hans Lody, alias Charles Inglis, caught the public's imagination. Lody was convicted and executed; according to a German paper quoted in *The Times*, he was shot.[163]

The spy scare was also a regional and local phenomenon. On 4 August 1914 the *Nottingham Evening Post* carried news about spies in Grimsby and Newcastle. The next day its readers learned about a pork butcher arrested in London. It was said that bombs and rifles were found in his shop. After that, there were stories of secret agents in places like Sheerness, Barrow-in-Furness, Newark, Conway, South Shields – a plague of spies. The epidemic reached Nottingham on 10 August with the arrest of Max Kühner, an employee of a local lace firm. It was reported that this 44-year-old 'big, powerfully-built man' had served in the German army, obtained useful information for the enemy, collected maps and possessed 'a fully-loaded' Browning revolver, which had been discovered in his bedroom. Kühner explained that the maps came from booksellers and that he represented his firm in South America, where everybody carried firearms for self-protection. After a week in prison it became clear that there was no evidence to prosecute Kühner and he was released. The police kept his revolver.[164]

Most espionage suspects were released without trial, and the spy mania seems to have subsided. However, the scare was accompanied and followed by violence against what the Conservative MP Joynson-Hicks called 'the enemy alien peril'.[165] Anti-German riots and disturbances were widespread in Britain, and the police made thousands of arrests for public order and looting offences. The main unrest took place in August, September and October 1914, May 1915, June 1916 and July 1917. London saw most of the early rioting, but the unrest of the first three months also reached other cities, towns and villages. In Worksop, Nottinghamshire, a brick was thrown at a German pork butcher shop. A crowd of about 5,000 people in Keighley, Yorkshire, apparently involved in a local labour dispute, let out their anger on three German butchers. A large mob ran amok in Crewe, Cheshire.[166]

The most extensive riots ensued in 1915. On Friday 7 May of that year German submarines sank several Allied ships, including the *Lusitania* off the Irish coast. The ship was sailing from New York to Liverpool, her homeport (the Cunard Line steamer had been built by John Brown & Co. in Clydebank near Glasgow). Over a thousand of her passengers and crew drowned. The *Daily Mail* published 'My personal view' by Lovat Fraser: The sinking of the Lusitania – after the asphyxiating gases with 'their slow and cruel torture [...] the orgy of slaughter and bestiality [...] inhuman outrages [...] innumerable vile deeds' on soldiers and citizens, 'men and women alike [–] shows the Germans to be a horde of mad dogs, and until they are settled with, life will never again be clean and sweet and safe'.[167] The rioting began on 8 May in Liverpool, where it lasted for several days, reached Manchester and Salford on 10 May, where it endured for a couple of days, and spread from there across the country.

The *Daily Mail* reported on 13 May about 'streets of pillagers [with] excited crowds [...] expressing their sense of the enemy-alien danger by wrecking the shops of all the uninterned Germans they were able to identify'. And 'frenzied [women] joined in with extraordinary fury and did more than their share of the destruction and the looting'. About the Smithfield market in London, the paper wrote: 'Germans were themselves responsible for the ugly and dangerous scenes' because they, despite warnings to stay away, drove up to obtain supplies at the market. In Aldgate 'another knot of German butchers were "chivied" down [...] by a stone-throwing crowd and several were injured'. Back in Smithfield one 'German was forced into a horse-trough to the yells of the crowd, "You drown women and children – now we will drown you"'.[168]

Yorkshire was seriously hit, particularly Sheffield, where looters, including many women, appeared keen on clearing shops of their stock. A local paper reported that the police

> were busy all through Friday night and Saturday in tracing the stolen property, and the results of their efforts [were] seen on Saturday morning when Attercliffe Police Station resembled an up-to-date pork butcher's shop. There were eight or nine hams, seven sides of bacon, boiled hams of tempting quality, pigs' faces and feet, half-a-dozen legs of pork, tubs and tins of lard, tins of pork fat, links of poloney, black puddings galore, brass weights, plates, dishes, potted meats and brawn and a host of other things.[169]

There was unrest in other Yorkshire towns, including Bradford, Rotherham and Doncaster. During an incident in Goldthorpe a shopkeeper who was wrongly regarded a German Jew allegedly fired shots. Five rioters were wounded (one of them fatally), and 17 men were sentenced from two to 15 months in prison. A judge in the Leeds Assizes blamed local 'miners [–] a fine body, but often thoughtless and childish'.[170] All over Britain the last but most furious disturbances took place on Saturday 15 May with the rioters attacking German shops.[171]

A Home Office abstract[172] records 1,374 claims made under the Riots (Damages) Act during the war in 24 police districts across England and Wales (but probably omitting the capital as there was only one entry on London City). They included 1,169 claims made by British subjects, 167 by alien enemies and 38 by others not listed as British subjects or enemy aliens. Most claims came from Liverpool: 625; then came Manchester: 120; Salford: 66; Leeds: 61; and Hull: 50. More than 10 but less than 50 claims arose in Birkenhead, Gateshead, South Shields, Southend-on-Sea, Newcastle, West

Riding, Rotherham and Sheffield. Leicester, Grantham and Warwick each lodged one claim.

As argued elsewhere,[173] local circumstances could prevent the outbreak of anti-German riots. For example, Glasgow was spared, but Greenock down the Clyde bore the brunt. In Glasgow the willingness, readiness and ability of local authorities to maintain order helped to prevent sustained extreme violence. Local factors could also influence the ferocity of the violence. The Home Office log mentioned above contained an entry on Nottingham, where three claims were made by British subjects (for a total of £36 6s. 9d.) and five by enemy aliens (£27 0s. 3d.). The eight claims therefore included a relatively high number of aliens. They totalled just over £63, low compared to other entries with a similar number of claims, which suggest that the rioters caused less damage in Nottingham than elsewhere, perhaps because the police undertook protective and crowd-dispersing actions that added to the limitation of violence. The police action was welcomed by the Nottingham political establishment and socio-economic elite, who most likely abhorred the public violence. A coroner dubbed the riots 'silly work'. And the Recorder of the City of Nottingham, Sir William Ryland Dent Adkins MP, declared at the Quarter Sessions:

> I regret to notice quite recently a very slight outbreak of that temper, of indignation, which has shown itself in some parts of the country; but I am quite sure that it is only a passing exhibition, and that in the city of Nottingham that attitude of stern and resolute self-control, which is the only proper attitude in these times, will be carefully and rigorously preserved.[174]

Across Britain[175] members of the local establishment occasionally defended Germans in Britain, writing in newspapers or speaking in public, reminding their audiences that some of these Germans had settled in Britain long ago, were naturalised and lived quietly and industriously among them. For example, a correspondent of the *Glasgow Herald* argued:

> First that the Germans in our midst are, in many cases at least, not here by their own wish, and would leave if they could; second, that those settled in this country before the war, whatever their private sentiments, cannot be regarded as effective members of the German nation responsible for the war; third, that in many cases relations of friendship on both sides have grown up between German residents and our countrymen; [and] fourth, that by any sort of social persecution of German individuals in

this country we shall distinctly fall below the level of Germany, which treated Britons in Germany with civility.[176]

And the former Lord Provost of Glasgow, Sir Daniel Macaulay Stevenson, declared in a public letter that the treatment of the German immigrants and their descendants in Britain was 'absolutely anti-British and contrary to all our traditions'.[177]

Also appealing to newspaper readers were reports about German nationals serving in the British army. One such story concerned Squadron Sergeant-Major H. W. Baker. After he died in action it was discovered that the man was German, when his widow read an article about a German woman, who had failed to register as an enemy alien and claimed she had a son who served as a Squadron Sergeant-Major with the name of Baker in the British army. She had brought him to England before he was 3 years old. Baker's widow, a Scottish-born woman, thus became an enemy alien through her marriage, but the Home Office restored her British nationality, which she received with the arrears of her pension.[178]

Germans in Britain also became victims of German military actions. In 1917 an inquest heard that among the 20 victims of a London air raid were Henry John Hoppe, a German journeyman baker, and Philip Franzman, a German baker who was naturalised 20 years ago.[179] This contributed to the confusion caused by the use of terms such as German, alien, enemy alien, friendly alien and neutral alien – with friendly referring to citizens of states allied to Britain in the war.[180] The House of Lords was told in 1916: 'Many people seemed to be unable to distinguish between nationalities, and so every friendly alien was regarded by them as a Hun.'[181] However, less than a year later a proposal was made in the Lords to substitute the word 'foreigner' with 'alien' in the Companies (Foreign Interests) Bill that was discussed at the time.[182]

In the final years of the war the word alien acquired a new connotation, which could be combined with existing associations. In 1918 a coroner blamed the panic at an air raid shelter, which caused 14 victims, including 6 deaths, almost entirely on 'persons who might be called foreigner, or who were of foreign extraction'. At the inquest, a police superintendent said he 'was amazed at the number of strong, able-bodied young men, nearly all aliens or of alien type, and it was these people who [had been] largely responsible for the trouble' by pushing people over, who were then trampled to death. Later it was said that places like Henley, Maidenhead and Slough had witnessed an invasion of aliens – who were considered to be a 'pest' – trying to escape the raids on London, and questions were asked in parliament whether to give

British women and children access to shelters before 'men of enemy and alien extraction'.[183]

Aliens were accused of draft-dodging and cowardice. Under the heading 'Aliens eating us out. Unrationed young Russians' a *Daily Mail* correspondent reported that in 'Bradford (where there are more Huns, naturalised and unnaturalised, than in any other English town out of London)' and in Leeds and Manchester 'rationing appeals [are] ignored by "friendly aliens".' Thousands of them could be seen in London's Shoreditch: 'In the teeming byways is an overwhelming preponderance of young Russian Jews having a very merry time.' A local councillor said that he had for months

> vainly attempted to move the recruiting authorities to rope in some of these fit young men [...] there are more than 6,000 young Russian Jews in Shoreditch living on the fat of the land [...] they also have snatched up the jobs of hundreds of young Englishmen who have had to go into the Army. Further, they are getting all the best-paid positions vacated by English workmen now fighting for their homes.[184]

In the summer of 1918 these feelings fed a campaign against the 'enemy alien peril' on issues such as the internment of all enemy alien males, repatriation of females, winding up German banks and disallowing alien banks. A national demonstration reportedly attracted the largest crowd to Trafalgar Square since the outbreak of the war. It demanded a 'clean sweep [–] intern them all'. During an anti-alien rally in Hyde Park, organised by the British Empire Union, the suffragette Norah Dacre Fox said she saw an 'open fight between the British public and German influence at work in this country'. There were series of meetings across the country, and a petition for interment of all enemy aliens received well over a million signatures.[185]

A new situation arose with the bolshevist revolution in Russia and Britain's intervention in the subsequent civil war on the side of the white armies, and it gave a new impetus to the connotation of alien with revolutionary violence. Not only seen as instigators, aliens were often portrayed as followers and therefore (potential) victims of radicalism. When the communist John Maclean decided to stand against a Labour candidate in the Gorbals constituency of Glasgow, *The Times* commented: 'The people [of the Gorbals] consist mainly of small tradesmen, hard-working trade unionists, a fair sprinkling of Irishmen, and a considerable colony of Jews, mainly of alien origin.'[186] In 1919, the House of Commons discussed alien influence in trade unions – 'foreign spies' were said to cause unrest. *The Times* reported a case in the Old-street Police Court, with connections to an East End gambling house, prostitution and a revolutionary club called Industrial Workers of the World, which distributed literature that, according to police a witness, was 'written with the idea of disturbing the workers here'.[187]

News on the role of immigrants in labour disputes had been reported earlier, notably in foreign news stories. In the United States immigrants had long been associated with trade unionism, radical politics – such as anarchism, socialism and bolshevism – and terrorism. The association with radical politics had been brought about by what was reported in Britain as 'labour riots'. In Chicago in 1886 a labour dispute about wages and working hours in the timber industry resulted in a meeting: 'Socialist leaders made some violent speeches to a crowd of about 1,500 persons, chiefly Bohemians, Poles and German anarchists.' When the police intervened, the report said a call 'To arms' went up and a bomb made of dynamite was thrown among the police officers, who fired their revolvers in response. Six policemen died instantly and 27 were seriously wounded, including some fatally. About 50 other people were killed and wounded. The report continued that later the police had discovered a 'Socialist armoury'. Similar labour actions and riots occurred in other industries and cities of the United States.[188] The next day further reports were made in Britain of 'Socialist riots', 'red flags' and 'relentless warfare' in the United States.[189]

The readers of *The Times* were given notice that similar events could happen in Britain when a month after the Chicago riots a cabinetmaker and secretary of the Bloomsbury Branch of the Socialist League was charged with causing an obstruction by assembling a mob. A policeman had threatened to arrest the secretary, asking him to get down from a chair on which he was addressing a crowd of about 500 people, but another man said: 'If this occurred there would be a repetition of the Chicago riots.'[190]

In later years, the German presence among immigrants and the immigrant influence in revolutionary violence became major topics in news stories from Canada. In 1918 *The Times* reported anti-alien riots in Toronto, which had been started by soldiers returning from the fronts of the First World War. A year later a correspondent wrote: 'It is conclusively settled that the object of the [alien] strike leaders at Winnipeg was to establish a Soviet and overthrow constitutional government.'[191]

The danger of these disturbances arising in Britain was reiterated in 1920 when *The Times* wrote about Cecil L'Estrange Malone MP, who had been sentenced for acts 'likely to cause sedition and dis-affection among the civilian population'. He was reported to have said: 'We are out to change the present Constitution, and if it is necessary to save bloodshed and to save atrocities we shall have to use the lamp-post [...] What are a few Churchills or Curzons on lamp-posts, compared to the massacre of thousands of human beings?' The MP had delivered his speech to an audience in the Albert Hall of 8,000 or

9,000 people including 'young alien East-End Jews of the disorderly type'.[192] Following publication of an article in *The Guardian*, the *Daily Mail* wrote about Malone and mentioned a letter from the suffragette and communist Sylvia Pankhurst to Lenin as proof of their subversion.[193]

Sedition was one of the issues mentioned during the consideration of new alien legislation in the Commons. Several Conservatives blamed labour and political unrest on aliens, linking immigration and subversion. By 1920 all reports in *The Times* on political violence were related to bolsheviks, communists or 'Reds'.[194] On the murder of the tsar and his family the paper wrote: 'Their guards, at first, were Russians, who, brutal as they were, never attained the fiendish ingenuity that came to be displayed by the alien guards and executioners of the final week.'[195] And on bolshevist propaganda in England: 'It is remarked that not only in London, but in Manchester and Glasgow, a large number of the Soviet agitators are aliens, and many of them alien Jews.'[196]

A physical difference was discerned that tarnished alien revolutionaries. In a report called 'Holiday making in the park', *The Times* wrote about the May Day procession and festival in Hyde Park: 'A well dressed, well fed crowd is always well conducted and orderly, and Saturday's crowd, conscious of its smart good looks, was perhaps the most orderly of any that has ever assembled in the great park. In its multitude of pink faces the small and swarthy alien element seemed lost, outnumbered and outclassed by the predominant type.'[197] Calling aliens dark-skinned evoked the already mentioned connotation of aliens being of a different race than the British race, as was expressed during the Tiger Bay riot, where it was accompanied by the portraying of aliens as sexual assaulters of British women, an image that had been painted earlier about Chinese men. In the new picture, aliens were again given a skin colour that was supposed to distinguish them from Britons.

However, during this period it was mostly the First World War that caused the very large rise in the use of the word alien, and it was largely connected to Germans in Britain, who suffered in varying degrees from wartime regulations, public distrust and violence. Local factors influenced public opinion about aliens living in these locations and changed expressions of anti-alien feeling. In London and other English towns and cities aliens, including friendly aliens, were accused of draft-dodging, profiteering and cowardice. And nationally, the word peril, which had been previously reserved for Chinese men, was applied to German aliens. Finally, a renewed association of all aliens and political violence was made by accusing them of bolshevist subversion and revolution.

Thus, by 1921, to contemporary ears alien sounded more hostile than foreigner. In 1918 *The Times* agreed with a correspondent who protested about the application of the word alien to French people: 'It is associated […] with a significance which is absent from "Frenchman" or "foreigner" [...] and is better relegated at once to the categories of enemies and neutrals.' The same editorial stated that Americans also detested 'the use of the word and its implications'. A day later a Belgian correspondent declared 'my countrymen feel very sorry to be called alien'.[198] During the next year, the Foreign Press Association, working with the National Service Department to encourage the enlistment of its members was said to have brought 'about an innovation by which [these members] were to be called foreigners and not "aliens".'[199]

In summary, the label of alien could be assigned singly or simultaneously to people from different parts of the United Kingdom such as the Irish, Scots and Welsh. It could also be applied to people from foreign countries such as France, Italy, Germany, Russia and Poland, the United States and China. And to population groups such as Jews, Lascars and Gypsies. Or to immigrants in general.

Immigrants could be hard-working or wealthy, but by 1890 these aliens were largely regarded as undesirable invaders, with connotations that could be evoked randomly or systematically, separately or jointly – it was felt they were paupers, disease carriers, cheap labourers, job and housing thieves, petty criminals, vice pedlars, seducers and groomers, murderers and terrorists. Their presence was increasingly seen as a threat to what was perceived as a British race. By 1921 aliens were associated with roughness, destitution, disease, physical and mental ill-health, fraud, unfair competition, general bad behaviour, violence, crime, terrorism, sexual exploitation and deviation, cowardliness and revolutionary politics.

This development ran through several stages and was influenced by different factors. Before 1861 aliens did not make the headlines often. Between 1861 and 1880 they were more often in the news, but only occasionally as immigrants in Britain, when they were accused of having committed the first terrorist acts on British soil or mentioned as settlers in overcrowded areas such as the East End of London, which became a focus of attention after 1881. This caused anti-alien agitation, which was fuelled partly by reports on immigrants in former and existing British colonies, and this agitation contributed to a parliamentary debate about restriction of alien immigration, resulting in the Aliens Act of 1905. In times of conflict, such as the Second South African War and the First World War, 'alien' got an outright hostile connotation. As a result of this development the label alien could be attached at will or unconsciously to immigrant groups that caught people's attention, and in some instances the marker occurred with menacing non-British traits and threatening ethnic attributes.

CONCLUSION

This book set out to review changes in attitudes towards immigrants in Britain and the language that was used to put the changing feelings into words between 1841 and 1921. It examined the use and the meanings of the word alien in that period, the overtones it bore and what people meant or felt when they applied it. This study drew on dictionary and newspaper sources and analysed them within a context of census reports, parliamentary records and other publications, with the help of the existing historical and linguistic literature, in order to gain a greater understanding of how opinions about immigrants came about in a modern West European country.

This is of course not the ultimate work on its subject; it was written to encourage further debate and publication in order to clarify, broaden and deepen our appreciation of the process of integration of immigrants and their descendants into Western societies. To achieve that aim much more work remains to be done and the conclusions drawn here only have a limited and provisional character.

However, using a historical and linguistic method for an analysis, of so far relatively unused primary sources, this book offers some novel findings. It has found that changes in the meaning and use of the word alien in Britain coincided during the period between 1841 and 1921 with the expression of changing attitudes towards immigrants in this country and the modification of the British variant of the English language. When people in Britain during these years used the term an alien, they meant most likely a foreigner, stranger, refugee or immigrant. More specifically, in 1841 an alien denoted a foreigner or a stranger, notably a person residing or working in a country who did not have the nationality or citizenship of that country. By 1921 an alien mainly signified an immigrant in Britain. In 1841, in the sense of being foreign, alien already had various, and sometimes negative, connotations, for example, invoking hostility and repugnancy, but the word had not yet acquired its modern meanings such as unfamiliar, unlikeable and frightening.

In general, the use of the word alien in Britain rose significantly between 1841 and 1921, particularly at the end of the nineteenth century and the beginning of the twentieth century. Sometimes the rise of alien appeared at the cost of alternatives for that word, such as foreigner, which was used relatively less by 1921. At the start of the period under review, immigrants were present in Britain, but they were rarely discussed, and when they were mentioned, they were most likely called foreigners. By the end of the period immigrants were discussed much more often, but on comparatively few occasions with the use of the word foreigner; instead, when immigrants were mentioned, the use of alien had greatly overtaken the application of foreigner.

Although overall used less than alien, the word immigrant was also mentioned much more often in the early twentieth century than in 1841. It is possible that the rises in the use of alien and immigrant were related to the growing number of people living in Britain who had not been born there, which was first recorded in the census in 1841, became apparent to the public after 1881 and rose even more noticeably between 1891 and 1901. However, percentage wise immigrants remained a very small group in the total British population – only in a few boroughs in a handful of major cities did their presence substantially alter the composition of the population. Nevertheless, after 1881, immigration became the subject of an intermittent public and political debate, and in this debate the word alien became a standard feature.

There was no government policy or other official strategy between 1841 and 1921 to promote the use of the word alien. And there is no evidence to suggest that in official documents alien was used in other ways than to indicate – as a legal concept – a person who did not possess British nationality or citizenship. So the change from foreigner to alien was caused by other factors.

These factors came into play during a period when the wider British society went through a process of significant and gradual but sometimes abrupt transformation, for example, in terms of demography, economy, politics and identity: the population grew; cities mushroomed; transport became faster; new inventions made keeping in touch easier; literacy grew; commerce was reshaped; industrial production was mechanized; business opportunities arose; financial crises emerged; electorates were widened and increased; the role of the state grew; wars broke out; and for many Britons life changed completely, sometimes within one generation and that change was not always welcomed. How people in Britain saw themselves and formulated their identity also changed, and as self-images changed, the perception of other people changed too.

As stated, the use of the word alien rose, notably after 1880, and this apparently happened at the expense of other meanings and the use of synonyms, notably that of foreigner. As a label, alien could be assigned to different groups of people, initially solely to foreigners, but then also to persons from different parts of the UK such as the English, Irish, Scots and Welsh, and after that again to individuals from foreign countries such as France, Italy, Germany, Russia and Poland, the United States and China, and to entire ethnic groups such as Jews, Lascars and Gypsies – and increasingly to immigrants: foreign individuals and groups who resided in Britain rather than abroad. It was assigned to these people as they played a role in events and developments that drew public attention. In this way, over the years, alien acquired connotations of roughness, destitution, disease, physical and mental ill-health, fraud, unfair competition, general bad behaviour, violence, crime, terrorism, sexual exploitation and deviation, cowardliness and revolutionary politics.

These associations came piecemeal. For example, between 1861 and 1880 aliens were accused of having committed murder and terrorist acts on British soil. After 1880, following recurring economic downturns, the reported poverty, lack of sanitation and overcrowding allegedly caused by aliens in areas such as the East End of London became the focus of public attention, as did their competition in the labour market, which was often deemed unfair. Between 1881 and 1890, the changed meaning of the term an alien as an immigrant in Britain was established, with almost all the negative connotations it acquired before 1921. Following the culmination of the public and political debates in Britain on immigration in the Aliens Act of 1905, specific groups were caught in the limelight, including Gypsies, Chinese, Lascars, Jews and Germans, who were all also randomly credited with being the heralds of unwanted social changes, carrying non-British ethnic traits, sexual perversion and extreme political convictions. By 1921 the word alien aroused utter hostility in contemporary minds. Alien first became a byname for immigrant, then it turned into a term of abuse, a badge of dishonour and a mark of danger.

It is possible that in 1841, a negative concept about foreigners who had settled in Britain already existed in the native British psyche, but perhaps the idea lay dormant, was wakened after 1881 and rose quickly in times of rapid change, crisis and war, when it took the form of the alien. The development of the connotations of the word alien was not, or only in a minor way, caused by interaction between the native population and aliens; it was propelled by news reports on foreigners in Britain, and directed by fear about the wider changes in British society. Real or phantom threats materialized – population pressures grew, new economic problems arose, poverty and unemployment spread, defeat in war loomed, revolution threatened and physical degeneration lurked. As news and opinions spread faster, the idea of race came to define identity, with people from presumed foreign, that is alien, races supposedly endangering British society and nationhood. In these circumstances, state intervention became acceptable, as when the government and a majority of parliament intervened in 1905 with an attempt to restrict immigration in the form of the Aliens Act.

So, the connotations of alien, which were fuelled by the fear of a menace to what was regarded as the British way of life or the British race, got a quasi-official status. The anti-alien feeling was also powered by news about developments in former and existing colonies of the British Empire. Colonial legislation to restrict immigration or political strategies in overseas areas and countries to stop the entry and settlement of specific groups of migrants were not followed slavishly in Britain, but they did inspire negative feelings about aliens and offered examples of measures that could be taken. In all this, the effects of war – notably the Second South African War and the First World War – were acutely felt, and gave the word alien an even more hostile feel as the aliens in Britain seemed to hamper the British war effort.

The alien legislation, which was passed following the Second South African War and was replaced by the alien laws of the First World War, most likely caused the census use of the word alien in 1921, but there was more. Between 1841 and 1921 British English also changed and this too affected the changing use of alien. The transformation of the wider British society coincided with and accelerated the standardization of the British English language. In this linguistic process a more generalized perception of the original meaning of alien seems to have arisen – broader than the traditional legal concept of somebody in Britain who did not have the British nationality or citizenship. This perception spread across Britain during the period under review.

In 1841 the word alien was used widely with various meanings in everyday language. Towards the end of the nineteenth century it was increasingly and narrowly applied in the debate that discussed immigrants in Britain, more often than not in negative terms – the meaning of alien was therefore subject of pejoration. As the standard variety of British English was adopted in much of UK, the degraded meaning of alien and its connotations circulated quickly and widely. Alien not only replaced foreigner, meaning immigrant, but it also sounded more negative and distinctive than its alternatives, for example, an alien pauper was not just a foreign or immigrant pauper; it was a distinctly different, that is a non-British pauper.

However, there were dissenting voices. From 1880, *The Times* opposed anti-Semitism, the newly organized form of hatred of the Jews, who formed a large section of the immigrants in Britain. In 1892, Israel Zangwill sympathetically portrayed immigrant life in his novel *Children of the Ghetto*. In 1901, *The Times* described alien immigrants as being industrious and frugal workers. During the same year, and again later, the paper tried to offer a balanced view on immigration, for instance, stating that the accusation of the high number of aliens being responsible for lowering wages and standards of living had been proven to be an exaggeration. Some politicians shared these unbiased views. Stuart Samuel, MP for Whitechapel, argued during the debate of the

CONCLUSION

Aliens Bill in 1905 that immigrants were not a burden on public funds and that allegations made against aliens were not based on facts. With the Aliens Act of 1905, the majority of parliament and the government also guaranteed the right of asylum, for example, for people fleeing from persecution abroad. In 1909, Home Secretary Herbert Gladstone corrected Judge James Rentoul on his assertion about a high number of criminals being aliens. In 1915, the Recorder of the City of Nottingham, Sir Ryland Adkins MP, condemned the anti-German riots. A year later the former Lord Provost of Glasgow, Sir Daniel Macaulay Stevenson, declared the war-time treatment of Germans in Britain contrary to all British traditions.

Nevertheless, attitudes towards immigrants changed significantly in Britain between 1841 and 1921, and this was accompanied by the increasing use of the word alien. The issues were related: the worsening attitudes helped to bring about the greater use of alien; and the greater use of alien helped to worsen the attitudes. In other words, at the same time language defined the experience of a changing world and emotion shaped word use. This relationship was also influenced by other factors, such as the transformation of British society, developments in former and existing colonies of the British Empire, and wider language changes, notably the standardization of British English, which all contributed to make 'alien' in 1921 a comprehensively negative label that could be attached at will or unconsciously at any time to any group of immigrants.

Migration is as old as humanity. It preceded 1841 and continued after 1921, leading regularly to what was deemed a 'migration crisis'.[1] Often, the number of immigrants arriving in Britain was viewed as alarming. Right up to the present day, newspapers reported new records, for example, *The Times* in 2022 writes about migrants crossing the Channel in the previous year: 'the annual total hit a record'; two months earlier the paper applied the fear-evoking word 'surge'.[2]

The post-1918 alien legislation in Britain put up hurdles for immigration,[3] but these barriers failed to stop it. The laws did not affect people coming from, for example, the British Empire or the newly independent states who joined the Commonwealth of Nations. An example were the Cypriots, who settled in Britain in larger numbers than before 1921. They were not regarded as aliens, but their growing presence made them a subject of public and police attention in the late 1920s.[4] Refugees became another noticeable group during the interwar period, including Jews and other people who fled from European countries such as Spain or Germany, Italy and Austria as well as Czechoslovakia and other states occupied by the Nazis. After the Second World War they were joined by Poles and Ukrainians, who did not return home, and, in 1956, by Hungarians who fled their country. Immigrants from former British colonies continued to arrive to the present day. For example, during the 1950s many people were attracted from the West Indies and the Indian subcontinent, including the 'Windrush' migrants from the Caribbean, Sikhs from the Punjab, Muslims from Pakistan and Hindus from India. The flow of Indian migrants to Britain peaked later with the arrival of people with Asian backgrounds from Uganda and other parts of Africa. They were followed by refugees from Bangladesh and Vietnam, and asylum seekers from war zones in the Balkans, the Middle East, Africa and Asia, and economic migrants from across the globe, notably from countries in the European Union.

Population movement is often experienced as a problem.[5] Immigration has once again become a divisive political issue in the United States and European countries, including the UK. The word alien has crept back in. A recent editorial in *The Times* states: 'There is in British society [...] a belief that Muslims are alien interlopers in western societies'.[6] In debates in English-speaking countries phrases are used such as 'illegal immigrant' and 'illegal alien'.[7] While 'child refugees' and 'people leaving Hong Kong' may be viewed favourably,[8] confusion reigns in the media about terms such as migrants, refugees and asylum-seekers, which easily get negative connotations, for example, in 'bogus asylum-seeker' and 'economic migrant'.[9]

The degrading terms not only denote people who come to a country in violation of the immigration laws of that country or continue to live there without residency rights, but they also express contempt, which is often prejudiced. It seems as if many people have an innate fear of other people. As if they are subconsciously biased against persons who look and act different. Perhaps this predisposition forms one of a multitude of factors that contribute to a sense of identity and self-preservation. In any case, this book has examined how and why expressions of that bias came out in the open in Britain between 1841 and 1921. Knowing this history may well make us realize that only understanding the immigration problem in full, not just foolishly labelling people, will help solve it.

NOTES

Preface to the 2022 Edition

1   See, for example, *The Times*, 19 November 2021 and 1 January 2022.

Introduction

1   See, for example, *Census of England and Wales 1911. County of Nottingham*, 65; *Census of England and Wales. 1921. County of Nottingham*, 58.
2   *Census of England and Wales. 1921. County of Nottingham*, xxxv.
3   Culminating in the 1979 première of Ridley Scott's film *Alien*, in which a particularly nasty and destructive creature bursts from the helpless body of Executive Officer Kane.
4   *Census of England and Wales 1911*, Birthplaces, England and Wales, vol. ix, Table I. Birthplaces of persons, males, and females, and proportions per 100,000 of the total population of each sex, 1911.
5   Pioneering studies include the following: Alderman and Holmes, *Outsiders and Outcasts*; Fishman, *East End 1888*; Garrard, *The English and Immigration 1880–1910*; Holmes, *John Bull's Island*; Holmes, *A Tolerant Country?*; Kushner, *The Battle of Britishness*; Kushner and Lunn, *Traditions of Intolerance*; Lunn, *Hosts, Immigrants and Minorities*; Panayi, *Immigration, Ethnicity and Racism in Britain 1815–1945*; Panayi, *Migrant City*; Porter, *The Refugee Question in Mid-Victorian Politics*; Walvin, *Passage to Britain*; Winder, *Bloody Foreigners*. It does not lie in the scope of this book to review the entire body of work on immigration in Britain. For a recent and comprehensive study and historiography, see Panayi, *An Immigration History of Britain*.
6   One of the first major studies is Gainer, *The Alien Invasion*.
7   See for example, Gainer, *The Alien Invasion*, 118; Lipman, *A History of the Jews in Britain since 1858*, 73.
8   See, for example, Bashford, 'Immigration Restriction'; Bashford and McAdam, 'The Right to Asylum; Bashford and Gilchrist, 'The Colonial History of the 1905 Aliens Act'.
9   Byrne, 'The Language of Migration in the Victorian Press'.
10 Baugh and Cable, *A History of the English Language*; Culpeper, *History of English;* Fennell, *A History of English*; Görlach, *English in Nineteenth-Century England*; Knowles, *A Cultural History of the English Language*; Leith, *A Social History of English*; McIntyre, *History of English*; Smith, *An Historical Study of English*.
11 For overviews of the changes in the wider British society: Ackroyd, *Dominion*; Heffner. *High Minds*; Davies, *The Isles*; Robbins, *Nineteenth-Century Britain*; Vernon, *Modern Britain*.
12 It was not until after the Second World War that immigration into Britain rose significantly, although for the remainder of the twentieth century the percentage of the population of England and Wales that was born abroad remained under 8 per cent; by 2011 it had become more than 12 per cent.

13 Panayi, *An Immigration History of Britain*, 1–36. For immigration in Scotland, see Braber, 'The Influence of Immigration on the Growth, Urban Concentration and Composition of the Scottish Population 1841–1911'; Braber, 'Immigrants'.
14 Panayi, *An Immigration History of Britain*, 37.
15 *Census of England and Wales, 1901. General Report, with Appendices*, 140–41; Braber, *Jews in Glasgow 1879–1939*, 4; Hutchinson, *The Butcher*, 230–31.
16 *The Illustrated London News* from 15 February 1849.
17 Compare Davies, *The Isles*, 752–53. In 1917, at the height of anti-German hatred, the royal name was changed from Sachsen-Coburg and Gotha to Windsor. Previously, when H. G. Wells remarked the royal court was 'alien and uninspiring', George V reportedly reacted: 'I may be uninspiring, but I'll be damned if I'm an alien.'
18 Davies, *The Isles*, 812–20.
19 For a wider discussion of racism and immigration, see Panayi, *An Immigration History of Britain*, 200–58.
20 *Daily Mail*, 20 January 1905.
21 Davies, *The Isles*, 705.
22 For a recent monograph on this war, see Beckett, *Rorke's Drift & Isandlwana*.
23 Britain was defeated by the Boers during the First South African War (1880–81).
24 Robbins, *The Eclipse of a Great Power*, 37.
25 One of its rivals, the *Daily Telegraph*, possibly had a larger distribution in 1861 (which rose to about 300,000 in 1888), but it may have had less influence on the establishment than *The Times*, and in any case did not start until 1855. Unfortunately, reliable circulation figures are unavailable for the entire period under review. For an overview, see King. 'British Newspapers 1800–1860'; Parkhouse, *Memorializing the Anglo-Boer War of 1899–1902*, 44–69; Vernon, *Modern Britain*, 218–20; Wadsworth, 'Newspaper Circulation, 1800–1954'. Brake and Demoor, *Dictionary of Nineteenth-Century Journalism in Great Britain and Ireland*, 627–28, put the 1841 circulation of *The Times* at about 32,000, and state that it rose, but declined again during last part of the century. On *The Times*, see also Griffiths, *The Encyclopedia of the British Press*, 562–63; Woods and Bishop, *The Story of The Times*.
26 The number of pages in *The Times* is relevant because it affects the quantitative analysis. The digital archive of this paper is available for the entire period of 1841–1921 and a full quantitative analysis can be made in this book of the paper's use of alien during these years. The other selected papers were not published during some years in the period 1841–1921 or their digital archives are not available for the entire period, which makes a full analysis impossible.
27 Brake and Demoor, *Dictionary of Nineteenth-Century Journalism*, 596–97; Griffiths, *The Encyclopedia of the British Press*, 233–43. See also Griffiths, *Plant Here the Standard*.
28 Quoted in Wilson, *The Victorians*, 590.
29 Brake and Demoor, *Dictionary of Nineteenth-Century Journalism*, 157–58. Griffiths, *The Encyclopedia of the British Press*, 184–85, puts the 1902 circulation in excess of one million. See also Addison, *Mail Men*; Taylor, *An Unlikely Hero*; Taylor, *The Reluctant Press Lord*; Taylor, *The Great Outsiders*.
30 Brake and Demoor, *Dictionary of Nineteenth-Century Journalism*, 50–251; Griffiths, *The Encyclopedia of the British Press*, 305.
31 Beckett and Oldfield, 'Greater Nottingham and the City Charter', 260; Giggs, 'Housing, Population and Transport', 436.
32 Griffiths, *The Encyclopedia of the British Press*, 442.

33 At the time of research, 2019, other newspaper corpora had been or were created with new technology that prevented imprecision and allowed for more advanced searches, but they were not publicly accessible.
34 See, for example, *The Times* 20, 21 and 24 September and 11 October 1917 for an article series on contemporary Russia, which used three different meanings of the word alien, as in Jews are an alien race in the Russian Empire, the revolution had adopted forms that were alien to the character of the Russian people, and revolution was exploited by alien influences. Similarly, see *The Times* 2 February 18 for a report on a Jewish couple – potential aliens – who had become estranged and alien to each other.
35 For a recent overview of general problems with statistics, see Blastland, *The Hidden Half*.

Chapter 1 The Meanings of Alien

1 Available online to subscribers via https://www.oed.com.
2 Leith, *A Social History of English*, 69.
3 *Historical Thesaurus of English*, Glasgow: University of Glasgow, available via https://ht.ac.uk.
4 There is a vast body of work on this subject. Useful introductions and pioneering works: Anderson, *Imagined Communities*; Smith, *The Ethnic Origins of Nations*. More recent examples: Roeder, *Where Nation States Come From*; Smith, *Chosen Peoples*.
5 Samuel Johnson, *A Dictionary of the English Language*.
6 The quotations above are taken from the first two editions. Alien was not selected in Lynch, *Samuel Johnson's Dictionary*.
7 https://www.merriam-webster.com.
8 https://www.collinsdictionary.com.
9 https://www.dictionary.cambridge.org.
10 As the transitive verb to alien, it came from *alienare*.
11 French also has the verb *aliéner*, which refers to the transfer of property, as in one of the meanings of the English verb to alien, or it means to render hostile or alienate. Germans nowadays use the adjective *alien*, but this is a simple borrowing of the English synonym for extraterrestrial, while *Alieni* is applied in German as a plural for animals that coincidentally live outside their normal habitat. As will be discussed later, the lack of a specific term for an alien does not prevent countries where English is not the official language from having policies on what would be called aliens in English.
12 https://www.oed.com.
13 *The Times*, 26 October 1849.
14 'Index of Subjects: Edward III', in Riley, *Memorials of London and London Life in the 13th, 14th and 15th Centuries*, lxii–lxx. See also *British History Online*: http://www.british-history.ac.uk/no-series/memorials-london-life/lxii-lxx, 306). Edward III also issued other regulations that affected aliens, for example, in the London weaving trade.
15 Blackstone, *Commentaries on the Laws of England*; Edlyne and Jacob, *The Law-Dictionary*.
16 See Bashford, McAdam, 'The Right to Asylum: Britain's 1905 Aliens Act and the Evolution of Refugee Law'.
17 In subsequent years parliament occasionally discussed alien legislation. See, for example, *Glasgow Herald*, 28 June 1844 and 9 August 1844.
18 For reports on the debate, see *Glasgow Herald*, 17, 21 and 24 April 1848; 5, 8 and 15 May 1848 and 16 June 1848.

98   CHANGES IN ATTITUDES TO IMMIGRANTS IN BRITAIN

19 See also Panayi, *An Immigration History of Britain*, 63.
20 Davies, *The Isles*, 996. The right of entry was automatic to citizens. Non-citizens had to seek permission to enter, for example, through visa application.
21 *The Times*, 4 May 1910.
22 *The Times*, 26 August 1911.
23 For an overview, see Baugh and Cable, *A History of the English Language*; Culpeper, *History of English*; Fennell, *A History of English*; Görlach, *English in Nineteenth-Century England*; Knowles, *A Cultural History of the English Language*; Leith, *A Social History of English*; McIntyre, *History of English*; Smith, *An Historical Study of English*.
24 Foreigner from foreign, in French *forein* or *forain*; stranger from French *estrang(i)er*; non-native from native, from the Latin *nativus*; and immigrant after emigrant, from Latin *emigrare*. This leaves the word outsider, from outside, a combination of two Old Frisian words: out, related to the Dutch *uit* and German *aus*; and side, related to the Dutch *zijde* and German *Seite*.
25 As referred to earlier, in linguistics a loanword – a word borrowed from another language – is called an alien.
26 Leith, *A Social History of English*, 70–72.
27 Baugh and Cable, *A History of the English Language*, 301–3. A word can also be used for different things than the thing it represented initially, which is called colexification. For a recent study on colexification, see Jackson, Watts, Henry, List, Forkel, Mucha, Greenhill, Gray and Lindquist, 'Emotion Semantics Show Both Cultural Variation and Universal Structure'.
28 Görlach, *English in Nineteenth-Century England*, 93; Leith, *A Social History of English*, 76.
29 For a recent reassessment of this period, see Oosthuizen, *The Emergence of the English*.
30 Görlach, *English in Nineteenth-Century England*, 111; Finkenstaedt, Leisi and Wolff, *A Chronological English Dictionary*, 80.
31 Leith and Graddol, 'Modernity and English as a National Language'.
32 *The Times*, 4 May 1910.
33 *The Times*, 26 August 1911.
34 *The Times*, 4 May 1910.
35 For a recent overview of war-related issues and language use, see Kelly, Footritt and Salama-Carr, *The Palgrave Handbook of Languages and Conflict*.

Chapter 2 Quantitative Analysis of the Use of Alien

1 The website Online Historical Population Reports offers a facility to search digitised census documents (available via http://histpop.org). A search for the string 'alien' results in 86 hits from 1841 to 1921, including 33 from before 1921. Unfortunately, these hits do not always lead to the word alien. For example, the found result 'Index of names of places, England and Wales, 1841, page 549' does not contain a reference to an alien or aliens.
2 *Census Reports for England, Wales, Scotland, Ireland and Northern Ireland* (1841–1921).
3 *Census of Great Britain, 1851, Population Tables*, I. vol. I, xxv.
4 Also quoted in Hutchinson, *The Butcher*, 220.
5 Also quoted in Hutchinson, *The Butcher*, 221.
6 *Census of England and Wales, 1901. General Report, with Appendices*, 138–45.
7 See also Hutchinson, *The Butcher*, 229–34.

8   See, for example, *Census of Scotland, 1911, Report on the Twelfth Decennial Census of Scotland.* vol. III, ix–xvi.
9   *Census of England and Wales, 1921, General Report with Appendices,* 154.
10 *Census of England and Wales, 1921, General Report with Appendices,* 151–54.
11 Available via http://googlebooks.byu.edu/x.asp. For a general work on the statistical analysis of writers' words, see Blatt, *Nabokov's Favourite Word Is Mauve.*
12 An exact search in the entire British Newspaper Archive shows that the word outsider was used 1,129 times in 1841–50 and 21,958 times in 1911–20.
13 *The Times,* 10 July 1860. Ashley lost the case.
14 https://www.collinsdictionary.com.
15 An n-gram is a set of words, see https://books.google.com/ngrams/info.
16 Available via https://www.proquest.com.
17 Available via http://hansard-corpus.org. The scope of this book makes it impractical to examine all parliamentary records from this period and provide a detailed and comprehensive analysis of government policy, and therefore a choice has been made to limit the search to Hansard.
18 Plural of the Latin word *alienigena,* meaning alien.
19 British Library, Nineteenth-Century British Pamphlets, searched September 2019 via JSTOR, with results limited to 'content I can access'. The article was 'A Foreigner's Impression of America', in *Scientific American,* 69, no. 16 (1893).
20 *The Times,* 15 July 1890.
21 *Nottingham Evening Post,* 3 and 4 March 1903, *Daily Mail,* 4 March 1903. Vincent was formerly Director of Criminal Investigation of the Metropolitan Police Detective Branch, and MP for Sheffield Central.
22 See Wasserstein, *Herbert Samuel,* 88–90, 125, 181 and 204 for Herbert Samuel's opposition to and involvement in implementing the 1905 Aliens Act. Stuart Samuel was a banker and a prominent English Jew.
23 Hansard, 29 January 1902 and 10 July 1905.
24 The searches of the British Newspaper Archive, the Nineteenth-Century British Library Newspapers collection and the Gale collections were conducted or completed on 18 September 2019, when the Archive project was still incomplete.
25 Meanwhile, a search of the slightly overlapping British Library Nineteenth-Century UK Periodicals collection shows, between 1840 and 1900, 49 results for 'alien' and 22 for 'an alien' or 'aliens'. They include 'The Irish are Aliens', in *The Satirist* or the *Censor of the Times* (London), Sunday, 22 January 1873, 443, which stated that the Lord Chancellor (Lyndhurst) was not so far wrong as many supposed 'when he declared the Irish are all aliens' to everything like good government or national prosperity and peace.
26 Available to subscribers via *The Times* Digital Archives 1785–2012, Gale Historical Newspapers: https://www.gale.com/uk/primary-sources/historical-newspapers.
27 Publicly available via British Newspaper Archive: https://www.britishnewspaperarchive.co.uk. Unfortunately, for the period under review the archive only supplies records for the *London Evening Standard* until 1909, while the records for the decennium 1860–69 appear unreliable.
28 Available for 1844–1900 via British Newspaper Archive: https://www.britishnewspaperarchive.co.uk.
29 Available from 1878 to 1895 and from 1899 via British Newspaper Archive: https://www.britishnewspaperarchive.co.uk.

100   CHANGES IN ATTITUDES TO IMMIGRANTS IN BRITAIN

30   Available to subscribers via *Daily Mail* Digital Historical Archive 1896–2004, Gale Historical Newspapers: https://www.gale.com/uk/primary-sources/historical-newspapers.
31   The *Standard* editions in the British Newspaper Archive also include *The Standard* (1827–1909), The *Evening Standard* (1860–71) and *Evening Standard* (1920–22). Among the papers in the British Newspaper Archive that used the words foreigner and stranger between 1700 and 2018, the *London Evening Standard* is the second highest user after the *Morning Post*, a daily newspaper published in London. However, some of these digital records appear unreliable.
32   The results of a search for the string 'aliens' in the records of papers in the British Newspaper Archive include 'alien', 'an alien' and 'aliens', which makes them incomparable with *The Times* and *Daily Mail* results.

Chapter 3 Qualitative Analysis of the Use of Alien

1   This term was eventually expanded to cover other living creatures than plants. See, for example, *The Times*, 14 January 1911, for a reference to alien ancestry in English bloodhounds.
2   See, for example, Henstock, Dunster and Wallwork, 'Decline and Regeneration', 133, on barring foreigners – people from other towns – coming to Nottingham; and Renwick and Lindsay, *History of Glasow*, 80–81, on an anti-Jewish measure taken in Scotland.
3   See, for example, *The Times*, 2 February and 1 December 1841.
4   See, for example, *The Times*, 6 and 16 January 1841.
5   The relative low use in 1852 occurred in all meanings but remains unexplained.
6   *The Times*, 5 October 1841. See also *London Evening Standard*, 5 October 1841. This was not limited to political elections. The *Nottingham Evening Post*, 31 March 1879, wrote about an appeal against the election of Mr S. Johnston as a science scholar, on the ground that he was a statutory alien, and therefore by the college statute incapable of holding scholarship.
7   *The Times*, 8 October 1841.
8   *Glasgow Herald*, 14 December 1846.
9   Early references in this period are *The Times*, 23 December 1842 and 7 May 1847 with, respectively, a letter about the Irish and their poverty in Kensington or a report on unsanitary situations in English cities created by the arrival of Irish immigrants.
10   *Glasgow Herald*, 3 June 1844, see also 1 May 1846 for a plea to treat Irishmen in Falkirk 'not as aliens, but as brothers'.
11   *Glasgow Herald*, 29 April 1868 and 2 May 1868.
12   *The Times*, 1 March 1842.
13   *The Times*, 12 October 1881.
14   *The Times*, 5 June 1868. See also *London Evening Standard*, 17 February 1844; *Glasgow Herald*, 2 February 1864; *Nottingham Evening Post*, 14 October 1878.
15   *Glasgow Herald*, 20 June 1845. Compare *Nottingham Evening Post*, 3 October 1878: 'When Catholics began to assert their rights and to claim their inheritance, they found themselves looked upon as aliens and interlopers in the house that was their own.' For a wider review of this subject see Fraser, *The King and the Catholics*.
16   *Glasgow Herald*, 22 May 1848.
17   *The Times*, 1 September and 29 December 1841.
18   *The Times*, 7 July 1845.
19   *The Times*, 6 June 1848. See also *The Times*, 23 July 1849.

20 *The Times*, 3 September 1849, 26 October 1849, 30 October 1849 and 6 November 1849; *London Evening Standard*, 25, 27 and 30 August 1849, 1 and 8 September 1849 and 16, 25 and 26 October 1849 and 5 November 1849; *Glasgow Herald*, 10 September 1849 and 29 October 1849.
21 *The Times*, 14 November 1849. See also *London Evening Standard*, 13 November 1849. One of Dickens's later novels, *Bleak House*, featured a foreign murderess, namely Mademoiselle Hortense, a French maid.
22 For more details, see Mulholland, *The Murderer of Warren Street*. For wider studies on these refugees, see Freitag and Muhs, *Exiles from European Revolutions*.
23 *The Times*, 11 December 1854 and 4 January 1855.
24 See, for example, *The Times*, 16, 20, 24 and 25 February 1858 and 5 and 15 March 1858. Compare *London Evening Standard*, 20 January 1858, with a report under the heading 'The French Assignation Planned in Birmingham'.
25 *The Times*, 15 March 1858.
26 The matter was taken up in an anonymous letter writer in *The Times*, 18 March 1858 and discussed again in a report on 5 April 1858.
27 *The Times*, 13 April 1858.
28 *The Times*, 10, 12, 14, 15, 16, 17 and 19 April 1858. Orsini was convicted in Paris and executed. Some of his accomplices in the French capital received death sentences, others were convicted to hard labour.
29 See *The Times*, 28 and 29 December 1911 about an armed alien arrested in Hyde Park, who was said to have carried a loaded revolver without a licence, and a double murder allegedly committed by an alien with a knife and poker.
30 Quoted in Fishman, 'Tower Hamlets 1888'.
31 *The Times*, 9 March 1844. See also *The Times*, 9 November 1844.
32 *The Times*, 20 November 1841.
33 *The Times*, 5 October 1845.
34 *The Times*, 17 December 1847 and 15 January 1848. This was not the first time, see, for example, *The Times*, 26 February 1840, for a report on Jews as alien brokers in the City of London. Jewish disabilities were removed in 1858.
35 See, for example, *Glasgow Herald*, 11 and 14 February 1848, for a Commons debate on civil rights for Jews, in which the opinion was voiced that the Jews were aliens in Britain.
36 *The Times*, 20 January 1879 and 20 April 1920.
37 See, for example, *The Times*, 14 and 21 March 1867.
38 *The Times*, 28, 29 and 31 October 1864, *London Evening Standard*, 21, 23 and 25 July 1864; *Glasgow Herald*, 23 and 25 July 1864, 9, 11 and 24 August 1864, 6, 9, 16 and 19 September 1864.
39 *The Times*, 1 May 1866. See also *London Evening Standard*, 26 April 1866 and 6 April 1858; *Glasgow Herald*, 26 March 1879 and 27 August 1881. Samuelson held his seat until 1895, further expanded his iron works across Britain, influenced technical education, and was made a Baronet and privy counsellor.
40 *The Times*, 3 October 1865.
41 *The Times*, 4 May 1867.
42 *The Times*, 20 May 1867. Compare *London Evening Standard*, 28, 29 and 30 November 1865.
43 *The Times*, 11 January 1868; *London Evening Standard*, 6 January 1868; *Glasgow Herald*, 1 January 1868. For a wider perspective on the perception of terrorism, see Frank, *The Cultural Imaginary of Terrorism in Public Discourse, Literature, and Film*.

44 As stated earlier, the intended meaning of alien is not always clear. See, for example, *The Times*, 27 December 1869 on a tenant right in Ireland: 'a plant [...] transferred to an alien clime'.
45 *The Times*, 28 May 1875. See pages 5 and 9 for two reports on Tipperary with different names for candidates who were declared aliens. See also *The Times*, 10 February 1921, for a return of the connotation of aliens with Irish terrorism when *The Times* wrote about 'Alien Adventurers' – seven Sinn Fein members who were on trial for attempting to murder a police constable in Bothwell (Scotland). The judge said 'there had congregated in parts of Scotland an alien population who had not a drop of Scottish blood in their veins [...] They were cosmopolitan adventurers.'
46 *The Times*, 12 January 1867.
47 The claim of unfair competition had been made earlier. See *The Times*, 25 May 1842, for a report of a case in Court of Common Pleas about porters taking goods to the houses of aliens.
48 For the causes of geographical distribution, demography and economics of immigrants in Britain, see Panayi, *An Immigration History of Britain*, 88–113.
49 *The Times*, 1 May 1866.
50 See, for example, *The Times*, 22 November 1880.
51 See, for example, *Glasgow Herald*, 7 April 1848.
52 *The Times*, 16 October 1906; Garrard, *The English and Immigration*, 18; Hansard, 11 February 1893 and 2 May 1905.
53 *The Times*, 12 January 1911.
54 *The Times*, 23 April 1914.
55 *The Times*, 7 November 1901.
56 For an overview and different contributions, see Manz and Panayi, *Refugees and Cultural Transfer to Britain*.
57 *The Times*, 12 May 1882. See also *London Evening Standard*, 8 May 1882; *Glasgow Herald*, 8 May 1882.
58 Later, Joseph Conrad's novel *The Secret Agent*, written between December 1905 and May 1907, but covering an earlier period, mixed ideas about Fenian bombings, anarchists and alien immigration. See also Hampson, *Conrad's Secrets*.
59 *The Times*, 20 August 1884.
60 *Nottingham Evening Post*, 15 May 1879, 16 January 1903. See also *London Evening Standard*, 8, 9 and 10 January 1903.
61 *The Times*, 22 June 1886. See also *London Evening Standard*, 22 June 1886 and 17 July 1886, which wrote about 'a common and ill-governed house'. The *Glasgow Herald* and the *Nottingham Evening Post* appear not to have reported this case. The association of aliens with vice remained strong, they could also figure as prostitutes and have different nationalities. See, for example, *The Times*, 21 October 1901 and 14 February 1919 for a letter from a distressed vicar on alien immigration and a report on a female Italian brothel keeper.
62 *Glasgow Herald*, 23 January 1892.
63 *The Times*, 24 September 1887, *Nottingham Evening Post*, 30 March 1886, 6 April 1886. Later the issue arose again. In 1898 it was stated: 'The number of aliens who got on the register in Stepney is enormous.' See *Glasgow Herald*, 23 February 1898, 12 and 16 March 1898.
64 *The Times*, 19 May 1887.
65 See, for example, *The Times*, 25 December 1894.

66 *The Times*, 30 May 1887. The phrase 'alien pauper' was much older. It was used on 31 October 1828 by the *London Evening Standard*.
67 *The Times*, 8 December 1893. On White's earlier work, see also *London Evening Standard*, 19 February 1885, 25 and 31 March 1885; *Glasgow Herald*, 27 December 1886; *Nottingham Evening Post*, 6 December 1887. For recent assessments of his role, see Bloom, 'Arnold White and Sir William Evans-Gordon; Johnson, 'A Veritable Janus at the Gates of Jewry'.
68 *The Times*, 30 May 1887.
69 *The Times*, 15 July 1890. See also *Glasgow Herald*, 29 January 1898, which carried an advertisement for 'A Typical Alien Immigrant', an article by Arnold White. He often repeated his ideas, for example, in the 1903 article 'The Alien Immigrant' in the *Edinburgh Magazine*.
70 *Daily Mail*, 18 September 1902.
71 *East London Advertiser*, 3 March 1888.
72 *East London Advertiser*, 6 October 1888.
73 It was not the first time the phrase 'destitute aliens' was used in parliament. Between 1882 and 1890 it was uttered 14 times, 85 times in the 1890s, 40 times in the 1900s, and 7 times in 1910s. In 1886 the Society for the Suppression of Destitute Aliens was formed.
74 Hansard, 10 March 1887. See also Fishman, *East End Jewish Radicals*, 70.
75 Hansard, 10 September 1886.
76 Hansard, 10 September 1886.
77 Hansard, 6 September 1887.
78 Hansard, 24 February 1890 and 26 June 1890.
79 *East End News*, 21 February 1888.
80 Laws of Foreign Countries respecting the Admission and Continued Residence of Destitute Aliens, Parliamentary Paper N C. 5168, in The National Archives, Kew.
81 HO45/10062/B2386, National Archives, Kew.
82 *The Times*, 10 and 25 August 1891.
83 See also a separately collated issue: Windham T. W. Quin, 'The invasion of destitute aliens. Eastern European Jewish Immigrants', in *The Nineteenth Century*, 1892.
84 A. White, *The Destitute Alien in Great Britain*.
85 The quotes are taken from Fishman, 'Tower Hamlets 1888'.
86 Hansard, 20 March 1888. Colomb was one of the members of the Commons committee.
87 Perhaps harder but not impossible, see *The Times*, 6 October 1910 for a report on a speech by Balfour who used alien in the sense of different, distinct and opposed to.
88 *The Times*, 29 August 1891.
89 *The Times*, 29 August 1891.
90 See, for example, *Daily Mail*, 6, 8 and 26 January 1903. See *The Times*, 11 May 1912, for a later example of an allegedly cheating alien.
91 In November 1892 the medical journal *The Lancet* published a report 'Cholera and Destitute Aliens' (vol. 140, no. 3610). For later examples, see *The Times*, 26 August 1913 and 17 September 1913. The *Daily Mail*, 23 August 1913 spoke of a 'contagious horde'.
92 *The Times*, 8 December 1893, 10 July 1894 and 6 December 1895. Compare *London Evening Standard*, 6 April 1892 and 9 October 1895; *Glasgow Herald*, 26 August 1896; *Nottingham Evening Post*, 31 March 1892.

93 *The Times*, 25 December 1894, see also 18 July 1894.
94 Hansard, 24 March 1898, 23 May 1898 and 5 July 1898. The parliamentary debate was widely reported. See, for example, *Glasgow Herald*, 24 and 25 May 1898.
95 *The Times*, 11 July 1901.
96 *The Times*, 13 August 1903, see also *The Times*, 1 May 1905 and 4 July 1905, for the paper's opinion on the bill that became act in 1905.
97 *The Times*, 13 and 15 July 1901 and 26 November 1901. The last date concerns a letter from Samuel Forde Ridley, the Conservative and Unionist MP for Bethnal Green South West.
98 *The Times*, 22 March 1902.
99 *The Times*, 12 July 1904.
100 This had not escaped the British public. The *Glasgow Herald*, 14 and 16 December 1898, for example, reported on the expulsion of aliens from Prussia and the alien question in the German and Austrian empires.
101 Caestecker, *Alien Policy in Belgium (1840–1940)*.
102 For example: in the United States the 1875 Page Act, the 1882 Chinese Exclusion Act, the 1885 Alien Contract Labor Act and the 1891 Immigration Act; in Canada the 1897 Alien Labour Act; and in Australia the 1905 Contract Immigrants Act, which followed Chinese exclusion acts introduced from 1855 across the six Australian colonies. For reports on these laws, see, for example, *Daily Mail*, 24 November 1896; *The Times*, 16 February 1899. The *Daily Mail* said the Coloured Aliens Restriction Bill was 'designed to restrict the immigration of the dreaded Asiatic, and to preserve as far as possible "Australia for the Australians" [and] keep out the undesirable Hindoos, Chinese, and Japanese'. *The Times* quoted the British-born and Glasgow-educated Premier of Queensland, James Robert Dickson: 'Our policy will be to exclude all alien and coloured races whose introduction is not already sanctioned by law.'
103 Bashford and Gilchrist, 'The Colonial History of the 1905 Aliens Act', 409–37. See also Bashford and McAdam, 'The Right to Asylum: Britain's 1905 Aliens Act and the Evolution of Refugee Law', 309–50; Reinecke, 'Governing Aliens in Times of Upheaval'.
104 Bashford and McAdam, 'The Right to Asylum', 317.
105 Quoted in Holland Rose, Newton and Benians, *The Cambridge History of the British Empire*, 411. Colonial conferences had since 1887 discussed Asian migration, for example, from India, China and Japan.
106 For a report on the debate of this law, see, for example, *London Evening Times*, 26 August 1896.
107 *The Times*, 5 January 1897.
108 Hansard, 4 February 1897.
109 See, for example, *Glasgow Herald*, 27 and 28 May 1898, 7 June 1898, 7 March 1900 and 15 January 1900, *Nottingham Evening Post*, 14 June 1899, 3 October 1899, *Daily Mail*, 28 November 1911.
110 *The Times*, 29 April 1902.
111 Royal Commission on Alien Immigration. Report, Cd. 1742, vol. 1, part 2, Measures Adopted for the Restriction and Control of Alien Immigration in Foreign Countries and in British Colonies, Colonial Legislation, 35–36.
112 The reporting that evoked these feelings was not limited to *The Times* and the other selected newspapers. See, for example, the *London Evening Times*, 8, 9 and 10 January

1903, which wrote about 'the dregs of foreign countries'. The *Evening Express and Evening Mail*, 4 April 1903 mentioned 'destitute aliens', including 'lunatics or idiots' in Cardiff and elsewhere. On wider welfare issues, see Hayes, 'From Aliens to Asylum Seekers', as well as other chapters in Cohen, Humphries, Mynott, *From Immigration Controls to Welfare Controls*. The feared spread of diseases such as cholera and at the time still little understood mental illnesses – 'lunacy' – caused regular panics in the nineteenth century British society.

113   The issue had been discussed in parliament since 1889. It was brought up again by Howard Vincent in 1905.
114   *The Times*, 24 July 1903. The *London Evening Standard*, 4 December 1900 reported an earlier case of hooliganism that involved a Nathan Ostbaum. The *Glasgow Herald* and the *Nottingham Evening Post* appear not to have reported the case.
115   *The Times*, 11 November 1911.
116   Hansard, 10 June 1912.
117   *The Times*, 16 March 1911. Compare *Daily Mail*, 31 March 1909, with a report on aliens and prostitution, involving a deputation of religious leaders including the Chief Rabbi to Herbert Samuel at Home Office, who said much had been done, but not enough: 'In 1907 there were 309 convictions for living on the earnings of women, and during the three years the Aliens Act had been in force 152 disorderly housekeepers had been sent out of England.'
118   *The Times*, 11 May 1904.
119   *The Times*, 13 May 1904.
120   *The Times*, 1 December 1905.
121   Holmes, 'The German Gypsy Question in Britain, 1904–1906'. Gypsies had been a concern earlier. See *Nottingham Evening Post*, 22 September 1886 about 'a batch of Greek gipsies in Hull'.
122   *The Times*, 18 May 1906. The issue was raised earlier in Scotland by the Scottish Shipmasters Association, see *Glasgow Herald*, 25 June 1898:
123   *The Times*, 11 February 1909 and 13 March 1909. See also *London Evening Standard*, 11 February 1909. The *Daily Telegraph*, 11 February 1909, reported he had tried a Russian burglar, a Polish thief, an Italian stabber and a German swindler.
124   See, for example, *The Times*, 16 March 1911, for a report on the 'Clapham murder' and a mention of Morrison in a report on a new ghetto in the East End of London. The Morrison case was also reported in other papers, for example, the *Nottingham Evening Post*, 15 February 1911, 7, 13 and 16 March 1911. The Slater case was also reported in other papers, for example, *Nottingham Evening Post*, 4, 5, 14 and 27 January 1909, 5 and 7 May 1909.
125   Braber, 'The trial of Oscar Slater (1909) and anti-Jewish prejudices in Edwardian Glasgow'; Braber, *Jews in Glasgow*, 23–29. For a recent work on the Slater case, see Fox, *Conan Doyle for the Defense*.
126   The materials preserved from the original investigation and trial are in Scottish Record Office, AD21, vols 5 and 6, and HH16, vols 109 and 110.
127   *The Bailie*, 12 May 1909.
128   The *Edinburgh Evening News*, 7 May 1909, which was quoted in the *Glasgow Evening News*, 8 May 1909. For Stinie Morrison, convicted in 1911 for a murder on Clapham Common, and similar cases, see *Glasgow Evening Times*, 17 May 1909; *Glasgow Herald*, 17, 18 and 19 May 1909 and 13 April 1911; and *The Times*, 16 March 1911. See also Feldman, *Englishmen and Jews*, 282.

129 *The Times*, 25 January 1909, see also 26, 27 and 30 January 1909, and 3 February 1909.
130 The popular press reported the Tottenham case of 1909 extensively, and some newspapers, particularly the *Daily Mail*, attacked the Aliens Act 1905, blaming it for being too open and making it too easy to enter the country. See also Glover, *Literature, Immigration, and Diaspora in Fin-de-Siècle England*, 182–83.
131 *Illustrated London News*, 7 January 1911.
132 Pathé, London - Sidney Street Siege 1911, available via https://www.youtube.com.
133 *The Times*, 19 December 1911.
134 *The Times*, 27 December 1910.
135 *Daily Mail*, 5 November 1911.
136 See, for example, Hansard 20 April 1911 and 28 April 1911; *The Times*, 29 April 1911; *Daily Mail*, 6 and 12 January 1911 and 19 April 1911.
137 For overviews, see Benton and Gomez, *The Chinese in Britain, 1800 to present*; Price, *The Chinese in Britain*.
138 *National Review*, XII, November 1888.
139 *The Times*, 25 May 1876.
140 See Blackburn, 'Princesses and Sweated-Wage Slaves Go Well Together'; O'Day, 'Before the Webbs'.
141 *Daily Mail*, 15 October 1900. The Society also opposed Polish, Austrian, German, and Russian Jewish 'pauper-alien[s]'. See also *Daily Mail*, 15, 20 and 28 September 1900 and 13 December 1900. The opposition to Chinese crews lasted. *A Steadily growing menace* (1913) was a cartoon published in *The Seaman*, the newspaper of the National Sailors' and Firemen's Union. The image was used in publicity material for the election campaign of the Liberal candidate Joseph Havelock Wilson, the union's President.
142 *The Times*, 25 May 1876.
143 *Daily Mail*, 22 November 1905. It was a regular feature of this paper. For example, on 31 July 1903 and 24 September 1907, it reported protests from the European population of Transvaal against the 'constant influx of low-class Asiatics', adding 'Australia is equally determined to combat the Asiatic invasion', and on Canada it stated: 'the "Yellow Peril" is a reality upon the Pacific Coast. It would take a very short time indeed for British Columbia to be submerged by the Asiatic, if immigration continued to increase at the ratios of the past summer.'
144 *The Spectator*, 11 December 1897. See also *Edinburgh Review*, July 1899; *Daily Mail*, 8 November 1902. For an overview, see Prince, The Yellow Peril in Britain 1890 to 1920.
145 *Daily Mail*, 17 May 1904, 18 August 1904, 22 May 1908 and 6 June 1908. See also *Daily Mail*, 17 November 1909 for a re-introduction of 'The Yellow Peril' in an advert for the *Harmsworth Atlas* and its companion book *The Romance of the Atlas*, which stated that H. G. Wells had drawn an appalling picture of wholesale devastation by fleets of Oriental airships and aeroplanes. A letter in *Daily Mail*, 7 July 1911, on 'The Singapore Murder' claimed that the British public still feared 'The Yellow Peril'.
146 *Glasgow Herald*, 2 August 1900. For other mentions of 'The Yellow Peril', see also *London Evening Standard*, 20 April 1895; *Glasgow Herald*, 27 April 1895; *Nottingham Evening Post*, 26 April 1895.

NOTES

147 *Daily Mail*, 4 July 1900. See also *Daily Mail*, 13, 14, 17, 21 and 31 July 1900 and 8 August 1900. Japanese expansion was also portrayed as 'The Yellow Peril'. The danger was compared to a 'Mongol horde' invasion.
148 *Sunday Chronicle*, 2 December 1906.
149 *The Times*, 2 July 1907.
150 Holmes, *John Bull's Island*, 79.
151 *Daily Mail*, 5 October 1920.
152 For overviews, see Saunders, 'Aliens in Britain and the Empire during the First World War'; Panayi, *The Enemy in Our Midst*; Panayi, *Prisoners of Britain*. Anti-German actions and measures continued after the end of the war. See, for example, *The Times*, 16 and 17 December 1918, for reports on the Stonebridge Park Conservative Club resolving to exclude members and visitors 'of enemy alien blood, naturalized or unnaturalized' and the Ariol Rowing Club in Hammersmith admitting no persons of 'enemy alien origin'.
153 *The Times*, 24 August 1911.
154 Alderman, 'The Anti-Jewish Riots of August 1911 in South Wales'.
155 *Nottingham Evening Post*, 16 April 1903.
156 *Daily Mail*, 6 October 1916.
157 *The Times*, 23 April 1914.
158 *The Times*, 16 October 1914. Compare *Nottingham Evening Post*, 4 September 1914. There was sometimes also a connotation of these aliens being criminals. *The Times* on 16 October 1914 carried a small report about an arrested alien thief who had failed to register. See *The Times*, 25 June 1915 for a report on a forger (from Hungary) who had failed to register. This type of cases continued after the end of the war. See, for example, *The Times*, 16 December 1918, for a case against a German carpenter, who was sentenced to four months' imprisonment with hard labour and recommended for deportation for failing to register.
159 The term enemy alien or alien enemy had been used before. First recorded in 1579, it was mentioned in a report on a Commons debate on the French Property Bill, see *The Times*, 7 February 1794. The total use in *The Times* between 1794 and 1839 was 23. It appeared 12 times in *The Times* between 1840 and 1849 and twice between 1850 and 1859, and was used again in various newspapers after that, for example, in reports on the American Civil War. However, compared to the First World War this use remained relatively low.
160 *The Times*, 17 February 1915. See also *The Times*, 15 June 1915 which reported about aliens in England in general, not just Germans.
161 See, for example, *The Times*, 17 February 1915.
162 See, for example, *The Times*, 21 August 1908.
163 *The Times*, 31 October 1914 and 3 and 19 November 1914.
164 *Nottingham Evening Post*, 4, 5, 6, 7, 10 and 15 August 1914. The case was extensively and widely reported across Britain. Panayi, *Prisoners of Britain*, 47, mentions it, quoting from the *Londoner Anzeiger*, 15 August 1914, which named the suspect as Max Kulmer.
165 *The Times*, 25 June 1915.
166 Panayi, *The Enemy in Our Midst*, 224–57; Pennell, *A Kingdom United*, 109. See also Ilett, 'Beastly to the Germans'.

167 *Daily Mail*, 11 May 1915.
168 *Daily Mail*, 13 May 1915.
169 *Sheffield Daily Telegraph*, 17 May 1915.
170 *Nottingham Evening Post*, 24 July 1915.
171 *Nottingham Evening Post*, 21 May 1915.
172 National Archives, HO 45/10944/257142.
173 Braber, 'Within Our Gates'; Braber, 'Living with the enemy'.
174 *Nottingham Evening Post*, 17 and 22 May 1915. The recorder was the highest appointed legal officer of the Crown in Nottingham and Nottinghamshire.
175 *The Times*, 30 March 1915.
176 *Glasgow Herald*, 1 October 1914.
177 *Glasgow Herald*, 3 June 1916. Stevenson himself was a target of anti-German agitation. The shipbroker and coal exporter stood out in politics for his progressive Liberal ideas, some of which he had implemented during his tenure as Lord Provost from 1911 to 1914. There was also a family connection. His brother-in-law was mayor of Hamburg.
178 *The Times*, 6 December 1915.
179 *The Times*, 12 July 1917.
180 An early wartime mention of friendly alien can be found in a notice on insurance rates in *The Times*, 8 August 1914.
181 *The Times*, 14 July 1916. The remark was made by Thomas Wodehouse Legh, Lord Newton, a Conservative peer who served as paymaster general during the First World War.
182 *The Times*, 4 May 1917.
183 *The Times*, 2 and 26 February 1918 and 23 July 1918.
184 *Daily Mail*, 8 May 1917, for 'Job-snatching [Huns]', see 10 March 1917. Kadish, *Bolsheviks and British Jews*, 52, refers to a leader in the *Daily Mail* on 16 May 1917, called 'Aliens Eating Us Out'. This is possibly an article published on 7 May 1917 headed 'Bread-eating aliens'. On draft exemption, see also Braber, *Jews in Glasgow*, 33.
185 *The Times*, 22 July 1918. Dacre Fox also spoke at the Trafalgar Square meeting, as did Rudyard Kipling. For Dacre-Fox, see McPherson and McPherson, *Mosley's Old Suffragette*. See also *The Times*, 8, 9, 13 and 15 July 1918.
186 *The Times*, 28 November 1918, see also 14 December 1918.
187 *The Times*, 28 August 1919, see also 2 July 1919 and 12 August 1919.
188 *The Times*, 6 May 1886. See also *Nottingham Evening Post*, 15 January 1885 and 5 and 8 May 1886.
189 *The Times*, 7 May 1886.
190 *The Times*, 22 June 1886. The connotation in Britain of aliens and political extremism and violence was often evoked through foreign news reports. See, for example, *The Times*, 3 April 1919, for a report on South Africa with the heading 'The Bolshevist Poison'. Riots similar to the events in Chicago and other cities in the United States took place in Canada.
191 *The Times*, 10 July 1919. See also *The Times*, 7 August 1918.
192 *The Times*, 20 November 1920.
193 *Daily Mail*, 27 October 1920 and 3 November 1920. *The Guardian*, 27 October 1920.
194 See also Kadish, *Bolsheviks and British Jews*, 44. In comparison, the *Nottingham Evening Post* reported occasionally on 'bolshevik danger' but only in relation to events that

occurred abroad, and when it wrote about the 'Reds' it meant the Nottingham Forest football team.
195 *The Times*, 27 August 1920.
196 *The Times*, 11 October 1920. See also *The Times*, 12 August 1919.
197 *The Times*, 3 May 1920.
198 *The Times*, 22 and 23 July 1918.
199 *The Times*, 19 April 1919.

Conclusion

1 *The Times*, 19 November 2021.
2 *The Times*, 13 November 2021 and 1 January 2022.
3 This process continues. At present, the UK government is amending a Nationality and Borders Bill, which has also been called an 'asylum bill' (*The Times*, 7 December 2021).
4 See Smith and Varnava, 'Creating a 'Suspect Community'. Cyprus had been under British administration since 1878 and became a crown colony in 1925.
5 *The Times*, 20 November 2021.
6 *The Times*, 10 March 2020.
7 See, for example, *New York Times*, 22 July 2016.
8 *The Times*, 1 September 2021 and 1 January 2022.
9 See, for example, *Daily Mail*, 5 November 2011; *The Guardian*, 5 June 2018.

BIBLIOGRAPHY

Primary sources

Census of England, Wales, Scotland and Northern Ireland (Census of Britain, United Kingdom Census, 1841–1911).
Hansard.

Collections

Nineteenth-century British Library Newspapers.
Nineteenth-century British Pamphlets, British Library.
Nineteenth-century UK Periodicals, British Library.
British Newspaper Archive.
Gale Historical Newspapers, *The Times* Digital Archives, 1785–2012.
———, *Daily Mail* Digital Historical Archive, 1896–2004.
Google Books.
National Archives, Kew.
Scottish Record Office.

Lexicons

Online

Cambridge Dictionary
Collins English Dictionary
Historical Thesaurus of English
Oxford English Dictionary
Merriam-Webster Dictionary

Printed

Finkenstaedt, T., Leisi, E., and Wolff, D., *A Chronological English Dictionary. Listing 80000 words in Order of Their Earliest Known Occurrence* (Heidelberg, 1970).
Johnson, S., *A Dictionary of the English Language: In Which the Words Are Deduced from Their Originals; and Illustrated in Their Different Significations by Examples from the Best Writers to Which Are Prefixed, A History of the Language, and an English Grammar* (London, 1755).

Selected newspapers

Glasgow Herald (1841–1900).
London Evening Standard (1841–1909).
Nottingham Evening Post (1878–1921).
Daily Mail (1896–1921).
The Times (1841–1921).

Other printed sources

Blackstone, W., *Commentaries on the Laws of England* (Oxford, 1765).
Census Reports for England, Wales, Scotland, Ireland and Northern Ireland (London, Edinburgh, Dublin and Belfast, 1801–2011).
Edlyne, T., and Jacob, T. G., *The Law-Dictionary, Defining and Interpreting the Terms or Words of Art, and Explaining the Rise, Progress, and Present State of the English Law; Defining or Interpreting the Terms or Words of Art; and Comprising Copious Information on the Subjects of Law, Trade, and Government. With Considerable Additions* (London, 1809).
Holland Rose, J., Newton, A. P., and Benians, E. A. (eds), *The Cambridge History of the British Empire: Vol. VII: Part I: Australia* (Cambridge, 1933).
Riley, H. T. (ed.), *Memorials of London and London Life in the 13th, 14th and 15th Centuries* (London, 1868).
Royal Commission on Alien Immigration. Report, Cd. 1742, vol. 1, part 2, Measures Adopted for the Restriction and Control of Alien Immigration in Foreign Countries and in British Colonies, Colonial Legislation (London, 1903).
White, A., *The Destitute Alien in Great Britain. A Series of Papers Dealing with the Subject of Foreign Pauper Immigration* (London, 1892).

Secondary sources

Books

Ackroyd, P., *Dominion. The History of England*, vol. V (New York, 2018).
Addison, A., *Mail Men. The Unauthorized Story of the* Daily Mail, *the Paper That Divided and Conquered Britain* (London, 2017).
Alderman, G., and Holmes, C. (eds), *Outsiders and Outcasts. Essays in Honour of William J. Fishman* (London, 1993).
Anderson, B., *Imagined Communities. Reflections on the Origin and Spread of Nationalism* (London, 1991).
Baugh, A. C., and Cable, T., *A History of the English Language* (London, 2013).
Beckett, F. W., *Rorke's Drift & Isandlwana* (Oxford, 2019).
Beckett, J. (ed.), *A Centenary History of Nottingham* (Chichester, 2006).
Benton, G., and Gomez, E. T., *The Chinese in Britain, 1800 to Present. Economy, Transnationalism, Identity* (Basingstoke, 2008).
Blastland, M., *The Hidden Half. How the World Conceals Its Secrets* (London, 2019).
Blatt, B., *Nabokov's Favourite Word Is Mauve* (New York, 2017).
Braber, B., *Jews in Glasgow 1879–1939. Immigration and Integration* (London, 2007).
Brake, L., and Demoor, M. (eds), *Dictionary of Nineteenth-Century Journalism in Great Britain and Ireland* (London, 2009).

Caestecker, F., *Alien Policy in Belgium (1840–1940). The Creation of Refugees, Guestworkers and Illegal Aliens* (Oxford, 2000).
Cohen, S., Humphries, B., and Mynott, E. (eds), *From Immigration Controls to Welfare Controls* (London, 2002).
Culpeper, J., *History of English* (London, 2015).
Davies, N., *The Isles. A History* (London, 1999).
Feldman, D., *Englishmen and Jews. Social Relations and Political Culture 1840–1914* (New Haven, CT, 1994).
Fennell, B. A., *A History of English. A Sociolinguistic Approach* (Oxford, 2001).
Fishman, W. J., *East End 1888* (London, 1988);
———, *East End Jewish Radicals, 1875–1914* (London, 1975).
Fox, M., *Conan Doyle for the Defense. The True Story of a Sensational British Murder, a Quest for Justice, and the World's Most Famous Detective Writer* (New York, 2018).
Frank, M. C., *The Cultural Imaginary of Terrorism in Public Discourse, Literature, and Film. Narrating Terror* (London, 2017).
Fraser, A., *The King and the Catholics. The Fight for Rights 1829* (London, 2018).
Freitag, S., and Muhs, R. (eds), *Exiles from European Revolutions: Refugees in Mid-Victorian England* (New York, 2003).
Gainer, B., *The Alien Invasion. The Origins of the Aliens Act of 1905* (London, 1972).
Garrard, J. A., *The English and Immigration 1880–1910* (London, 1971).
Glover, D., *Literature, Immigration, and Diaspora in Fin-de-Siècle England: A Cultural History of the 1905 Aliens Act* (Cambridge, 2012).
Görlach, M., *English in Nineteenth-Century England. An Introduction* (Cambridge, 1999).
Griffiths, D. (ed.), *The Encyclopedia of the British Press, 1422–1992* (London, 1992).
———, *Plant Here the Standard* (Basingstoke, 1996).
Hampson, R., *Conrad's Secrets* (Basingstoke, 2012).
Heffner, S., *High Minds. The Victorians and the Birth of Modern Britain* (London, 2013).
Holmes, C., *John Bull's Island. Immigration and British Society, 1876–1939* (London, 1979).
———, *A Tolerant Country? Immigrants, Refugees and Minorities in Britain* (London, 1991).
Hutchinson, R., *The Butcher, the Baker, the Candlestick Maker. The Story of Britain through Its Census, since 1801* (London, 2017).
Kadish, S., *Bolsheviks and British Jews. The Anglo-Jewish Community, Britain and the Russian Revolution* (London, 1992).
Kelly, M., Footritt, H., and Salama-Carr, M. (eds), *The Palgrave Handbook of Languages and Conflict* (London, 2019).
Knowles, G., *A Cultural History of the English Language* (London, 1999).
Kushner, T., *The Battle of Britishness. Migrant Journeys 1685 to the Present* (Manchester, 2012).
Kushner, T., and Lunn, K. (eds), *Traditions of Intolerance. Historical Perspectives on Fascism and Race Discourse in Britain* (Manchester, 1989).
Leith, D., *A Social History of English* (London, 1997).
Lipman, V. D., *A History of the Jews in Britain since 1858* (Leicester, 1990).
Lunn, K. (ed.), *Hosts, Immigrants and Minorities. Historical Responses to Newcomers in British Society 1870–1914* (Folkstone, 1980).
Lynch, J. (ed.), *Samuel Johnson's Dictionary. Selections from the 1755 Work That Defined the English Language* (London, 2004).
Manz, S., and Panayi, P. (eds), *Refugees and Cultural Transfer to Britain* (London, 2013).
McPherson, S., and McPherson, A., *Mosley's Old Suffragette. A Biography of Norah Dacre Fox* (np, 2011).

McIntyre, D., *History of English. A Resource Book for Students* (London, 2009).
Mulholland, M., *The Murderer of Warren Street. The True Story of a Nineteenth-Century Revolutionary* (London, 2018).
Oosthuizen, S., *The Emergence of the English* (Leeds, 2019).
Panayi, P., *The Enemy in Our Midst. Germans in Britain during the First World War* (Oxford, 1991).
———, *Immigration, Ethnicity and Racism in Britain 1815–1945* (Manchester, 1994).
———, *An Immigration History of Britain. Multicultural Racism since 1800* (London, 2010).
———, *Migrant City. A New History of London* (London, 2020).
———, *Prisoners of Britain. German civilian and Combatant Internees during the First World War* (Manchester, 2012).
Parkhouse, V. B., *Memorializing the Anglo-Boer War of 1899–1902. Militarization of the Landscape: Monuments and Memorials in Britain* (Kibworth Beauchamp, 2015).
Pennell, C., *A Kingdom United. Popular Responses to the Outbreak of the First World War in Britain and Ireland* (Oxford, 2012).
Porter, B., *The Refugee Question in Mid-Victorian Politics* (New York, 1979).
Price, B., *The Chinese in Britain. A History of Visitors and Settlers* (Amberley, 2019).
Prince, G., The Yellow Peril in Britain 1890 to 1920 (thesis McGill University, Montreal, Quebec, 1987).
Renwick, R., and Lindsay, J., *History of Glasow. Volume I, Pre-Reformation Period* (Glasgow, 1921).
Robbins, K., *The Eclipse of a Great Power. Modern Britain 1870–1975* (London, 1983).
———, *Nineteenth-Century Britain. Integration and Diversity* (Oxford, 1988).
Roeder, Philip G., *Where Nation States Come From. Institutional Change in the Age of Nationalism* (Princeton, 2007).
Smith, A. D., *Chosen Peoples. Sacred Sources of National Identity* (Oxford, 2003).
———, *The Ethnic Origins of Nations* (Oxford, 1986).
Smith, J. J., *An Historical Study of English. Function, Form and Change* (London, 1996).
Taylor, S. J., *The Great Outsiders. Northcliffe, Rothermere and the* Daily Mail (London, 1996);
———, *The Reluctant Press Lord. Esmond Rothermere and the Daily Mail* (London, 1998).
———, *An Unlikely Hero. Vere Rothermere and How the* Daily Mail *Was Saved* (London, 2002).
Vernon, J., *Modern Britain: 1750 to the Present* (Cambridge, 2017).
Walvin, J., *Passage to Britain. Immigration in British History and Politics* (Hammondsworth, 1984).
Wasserstein, B., *Herbert Samuel. A Political Life* (Oxford, 1992).
Wilson, A. N., *The Victorians* (London, 2003).
Winder, R., *Bloody Foreigners. The Story of Immigration to Britain* (London, 2004).
Woods, O., and Bishop, J., *The Story of* The Times (London, 1983).

Articles and book chapters

Alderman, G., 'The Anti-Jewish Riots of August 1911 in South Wales: A Response', *Welsh History Review* 20 (2001), 565–71.
Bashford, A., 'Immigration Restriction: Rethinking Period and Place from Settler Colonies to Postcolonial Nations', *Journal of Global History* 9 (2014), 26–48.
Bashford, A., and Gilchrist, C., 'The Colonial History of the 1905 Aliens Act', *Journal of Imperial and Commonwealth History* 40 (2012), 409–37.
Bashford, A., and McAdam, J., 'The Right to Asylum: Britain's 1905 Aliens Act and the Evolution of Refugee Law', *Law and History Review* 32 (2014), 309–50.

Beckett, J., and Oldfield, G., 'Greater Nottingham and the City Charter', in J. Beckett (ed.), *A Centenary History of Nottingham* (Chichester, 2006), 253–84.

Blackburn, S. C., 'Princesses and Sweated-Wage Slaves Go Well Together: Images of British Sweated Workers, 1843–1914', in *International Labor and Working-Class History* 61 (2002), 24–44.

Bloom, C., 'Arnold White and Sir William Evans-Gordon. Their Involvement in Immigration in Late-Victorian and Edwardian Britain', *Jewish Historical Studies* 39 (2004), 153–66.

Braber, B., 'Immigrants', in T. M. Devine and J. Wormald (eds), *The Oxford Handbook of Modern Scottish History 1500–2010* (Oxford, 2012), 491–509.

———, 'The Influence of Immigration on the Growth, Urban Concentration and Composition of the Scottish Population 1841–1911', *Journal of Scottish Historical Studies* 32 (2012), 190–212.

———, 'Living with the Enemy: German Immigrants in Nottingham during the First World War', *Midland History* 42 (2017), 72–91.

———, 'The Trial of Oscar Slater (1909) and Anti-Jewish Prejudices in Edwardian Glasgow', *History* 88 (2003), 262–79.

———, 'Within Our Gates: A New Perspective on Germans in Glasgow during the First World War', *Journal of Scottish Historical Studies* 29 (2009), 87–105.

Byrne. R., 'The Language of Migration in the Victorian Press: A Corpus Linguistic Approach', slideshare.net/historyspot/the-language-of-migration-in-the-victorian-press-a-corpus-linguistic-approach.

Fishman, W., 'Tower Hamlets 1888', *East London Record* 2 (1979), 19–27.

Giggs, J., 'Housing, Population and Transport', in J. Beckett (ed.), *A Centenary History of Nottingham* (Chichester, 2006), 435–62.

Ilett, R., 'Beastly to the Germans: Germanophobia in the Workshop Area during the Great War', *Nottinghamshire Historian* 96 (2016), 21–25.

Jackson, J. C., Watts, J., Henry, T. R., List, J.-M., Forkel, R., Mucha, P. J., Greenhill, S. J., Gray, R. D., and Lindquist, K. A., 'Emotion Semantics Show Both Cultural Variation and Universal Structure', *Science* 366 (2019), 1517–22.

Hayes, D., 'From Aliens to Asylum Seekers. A History of Immigration Controls and Welfare in Britain', in S. Cohen, B. Humphries and E. Mynott (eds), *A History of Immigration Controls and Welfare in Britain* (London, 2001), 100–117.

Henstock, A., Dunster, S. and Wallwork, S, 'Decline and Regeneration', in J. Beckett, (ed.), *A Centenary History of Nottingham* (Chichester, 2006), 132–64.

Holmes, C., 'The German Gypsy Question in Britain, 1904–1906' in K. Lunn (ed.), *Hosts, Immigrants and Minorities. Historical Responses to Newcomers in British Society 1870–1914* (Folkstone, 1980), 134–59.

Johnson, S., ' "A Veritable Janus at the Gates of Jewry": British Jews and Mr Arnold White', *Patterns of Prejudice* 47 (2013), 41–68.

King, E., 'British Newspapers 1800–1860', *British Library Newspapers* (Detroit, 2007).

Leith, D., and Graddol, D., 'Modernity and English as a National Language', in D. Graddol, D. Leith, J. Swann, M. Rhys and J. Gillen (eds), *Changing English* (London, 2007), 79–116.

O'Day, R., 'Before the Webbs: Beatrice Potter's Early Investigations for Charles Booth's Inquiry', *History* 78 (1993), 218–42.

Reinecke, C., 'Governing Aliens in Times of Upheaval: Immigration Control and Modern State Practice in Early Twentieth-Century Britain, Compared with Prussia', *International Review of Social History* 54 (2009), 39–65.

Saunders, D., 'Aliens in Britain and the Empire during the First World War', *Immigrants & Minorities* 4 (1985), 5–27.

Smith, E., and Varnava, A., '"Creating a 'Suspect Community'": Monitoring and Controlling the Cypriot Community in Inter-War London', *English Historical Review* 132 (2017), 1149–81.

Wadsworth, A. P., 'Newspaper Circulation, 1800–1954', *Transactions of the Manchester Statistical Society, 1954–1955* (Manchester, 1955).

INDEX

Addison, Joseph 20
Adkins, Ryland 82, 93
Akers-Douglas, Aretas 38, 39
Aliens Act of 1905 1, 3, 5, 23, 24, 67, 68, 69, 70, 72, 74, 87, 91, 92, 93, 106n.130
Ashley, Fitzherbert 33

Baker, H.W. 83
Baldwin, Charles 13
Balfour, Arthur 71
Banbury 57
Barnes, Thomas 13
Barrow-in-Furness 80
Barthélemy, Emmanuel 54
Bernard, Simon 55
Birkelvitch, Fredel 70
Birkenhead 81
Birmingham 14, 40, 101n.24
Blackpool 78
Blackstone, William 22, 49
Blake, Claude 76
Blantyre 78
Bournemouth 7
Bradford 14, 81, 84
Briggs, Thomas 57
Burke, Edmund 63
Burke, Thomas 61
Burke, William 52
Butcher, John 38

Calcraft, Henry 63, 66
Cardiff 7, 78
Cavendish, Frederick (Lord) 61
Chamberlain, Joseph 53, 68
Churchill, Randolph 53
Churchill, Winston 74

Colomb, John 64
connotations 17, 20, 21, 25, 26, 27, 30, 56, 66, 70, 76, 87, 89, 91, 92
   cowardice 83
   crime 62
   disease 66
   housing competition 63
   immorality 62
   labour competition 59
   polical subversion 86
   positive 61
   poverty 56, 59, 64
   sex 76
   terrorism 59
   underclass 56
   vice 62
   violence 55
   'white slavery' 70
Conservative Party 5, 13, 14, 38, 39, 60, 63, 64, 65, 67, 70, 74, 80, 86, 104n.97, 107n.152, 108n.181
Conway 80
Cork 58
Coventry 14
Crackanthorpe Montague 68
Crewe 80

Dacre Fox, Norah 84
Daily Mail 9, 10, 11, 13, 34, 40, 42, 64, 68, 72, 74, 75, 76, 77, 80, 81, 84, 86, 106n.130
Daily Telegraph 96n.25, 105n.123
Davies, Horatio 39
Davies, John 20, 52
De Roux, Maria or Marie 54
De Valera, Eamon 53

Derby 14, 40
Dickens, Charles 54
Dickson, James Robert 104n.102
Doncaster 81
Dublin 27, 58, 61
Dunbar, William 31
Dundee 7
Durham 39

East End News 64
East London Advertiser 64
Edinburgh 7, 27, 52, 63
Edinburgh Evening News 73
Edlyne, Thomas 22
education ix, 4, 8, 29
Evans-Gordon, William 38, 39, 71
Evening Express and Evening Mail 105n.112

Falkirk 100n.10
Fenian Brotherhood 58, 59, 61, 102n.58
First South African War 11
First World War 1, 14, 33, 35, 36, 45, 77, 86, 87, 92
Forde Ridley, Samuel 104n.97
Forel, August 11
Forman, Thomas 14
Franzman, Philip 83
Fraser, Lovat 80

Galton, Francis 10
Gateshead 81
Giffard, Stanley Lees 13
Gladstone, Herbert 72, 73, 93
Gladstone, William 53
Glasgow 7, 14, 40, 63, 82, 84, 86, 93
Glasgow Herald 14, 40, 42, 52, 53, 72, 76, 82
Goldthorpe 81
Gordon, Charles 11
Goulding, Edward 74
Grantham 82
Greenock 82
Grimsby 7, 80
Gypsies 72, 87, 91, 105n.121

Hare, William 52
Harkness, Margaret (John Law) 65

Harmsworth, Alfred 13
Harmsworth, Harold 13
Havelock Wilson, Joseph 106n.141
Henley 83
Heymann, Lewis 61
Historical Thesaurus of English 12, 17
Hoppe, Henry John 83
Hornsby 7
Hull 14, 81, 105n.121

Illustrated London News 74
immigrants
    American 58, 61
    Belgian 61
    Caribbean 60
    Chinese 5, 74–77, 86, 91
    Dutch 61
    French 54, 55, 56, 58, 59, 60, 61
    German 57, 60, 61, 62, 66, 83, 91
    integration ix
    Irish 7, 52
    Italian 60, 61, 62
    Jewish 7, 39, 56, 59, 60, 63, 71, 91
    Latvian 73
    Lithuanian 61
    Polish 61
    post-1918 93–94
    Russian 61, 66, 70
    Swiss 54

Jacob, Giles 22
Johnson, Samuel 20, 26, 28
Joynson-Hicks, William 38, 80

Keighley 80
Kensington 100n.9
Kingston-upon-Hull 7
Kipling, Rudyard 108n.185
Knox, Robert 52
Kühner, Max 80

L'Estrange Malone, Cecil 85
Labour Party 5
Lascars 60, 72, 87, 91
Lawson, Harry 60
Lee, Arthur 70
Leeds 7, 8, 14, 81, 84
Leicester 14, 40, 82

INDEX

Liberal Party 5, 13, 14, 38, 39, 67, 106n.141, 108n.177
Liverpool 7, 8, 14, 57, 76, 80, 81
Lody, Carl Hans (Charles Inglis) 79
London 5, 7, 8, 9, 13, 14, 27, 31, 40, 49, 54, 55, 56, 57, 58, 62, 63, 64, 65, 70, 71, 72, 73, 74, 80, 81, 83, 84, 86, 114
  East End 39, 59, 63, 64, 67, 73, 84, 86, 87, 91
  Shoreditch 84
  Spitalfields 8
  Stepney 8, 38, 59, 74, 102n.63
  Whitechapel 39, 63, 74, 93
London Evening Standard 13, 40, 42
London Evening Times 104n.112
Lowther, James 60

M'Cafferty, John 58
Macaulay Stevenson, Daniel 83, 93
Maclean, John 84
Maidenhead 83
Manchester 7, 8, 14, 40, 58, 80, 81, 84, 86
Manning, Frederick 54
McKenna, Reginald 38
Moore, George 55
Morrison, Stinie 72, 105n.128
Müller, Franz 57

National Review 74
Newark 80
Newcastle 80, 81
Newton (Lord) 108n.181
Northcliffe (Lord) 13
Nottingham 1, 14, 40, 42, 43, 61, 62, 80, 82, 93, 95n.1, 95n.2, 96n.31, 99n.21, 100n.2, 112, 115
Nottingham Evening Post 14, 40, 42, 80

O'Connor, Patrick 54
Obstbaum, Nathan 70
Outram, George 14
Oxford English Dictionary 17, 28

Pankhurst, Sylvia 86
Parnell, Charles 53
Pearson, Charles H. 75
Phipps Shiel, Matthew 76

Rentoul, James 72, 73, 93
Rotherham 81, 82
Rothermere (Lord) 13
Royal Commission on Alien Immigration 31, 67, 68, 69, 70, 71

Salford 80, 81
Salisbury (Lord) 14, 67
Samuel, Herbert 39, 105n.117
Samuel, Stuart 39, 93
Samuelson, Bernhard 57, 60
Second South African War 9, 11, 12, 29, 69, 87, 92
Shakespeare, William 20
Sheerness 80
Sheffield 14, 81, 82
Shortt, Edward 38
Slater, Oscar 72
Slough 83
South Shields 7, 80, 81
South Wales 77
Southend-on-Sea 81
Stoke-on-Trent 14
Sunday Chronicle 76
Suseman, Abraham 49
Swansea 7

Terry, Lionel 75
The Guardian 86
The Illustrated London News 9
The Spectator 76
The Times 13, 22, 24, 27, 29, 33, 38, 40, 41, 42, 47, 49, 53, 54, 55, 56, 57, 59, 60, 61, 63, 65, 66, 67, 69, 70, 71, 72, 73, 74, 75, 76, 77, 78, 79, 84, 85, 86, 92, 94
Tiger Bay 78, 86
Tipperary 59
Tynemouth 7

Vincent, Howard (Charles) 38, 39, 60, 67, 105n.113

Wakefield 33
Walter, John 13
Warwick 82
Webb, Beatrice (Potter) 74

Webb, Sidney 60
Wells, H.G. 106n.145
West Riding 82
White, Arnold 63, 64, 65, 66, 68, 69, 103n.69
Wilkins, William 65, 68
Willesden 7
Wilson, Sarah 10

Worksop 80
Wyndham-Quin, Thomas 65

Yarmouth 62
Yellow Peril 75–76
Yorke, Albert 67
Yung, Kum 75

Zangwill, Israel 71, 92

www.ingramcontent.com/pod-product-compliance
Lightning Source LLC
Chambersburg PA
CBHW021833300426
44114CB00009BA/429